CHRISTMAS IN THE BIG IGLOO
True Tales from the Canadian Arctic

Edited and with an Introduction by Kenn Harper

Outcrop
The Northern Publishers

Design: John Williamson
House Editor: Rosemary Allerston
Illustrations: John Allerston

This book was designed and produced by Outcrop Ltd.
The Northern Publishers
Box 1350,
Yellowknife, Northwest Territories
Canada X1A 2N9

Canadian Cataloguing in Publication Data
Christmas in the big igloo
ISBN 0-919315-07-0

1. Christmas — Canada, Northern. 2. Christmas — Arctic regions. 3. Canada, Northern — Social life and customs. I. Harper, Kenn, 1945-GT4987.15.C39 1983
394.2'68282'097199   C83-091453-6

Selection © Kenn Harper
Design/Illustration © Outcrop Ltd.

Printed and bound in Canada

For Navarana

Editor's Note:

Over the years, different terms have been used to describe the native people of the North. Today, we say *Inuit* instead of *Eskimos*, and many of the selections reflect this.

However, it did not seem right to correct the language of people who were writing long before this usage became accepted. Therefore both terms occur in the book.

Acknowledgments

Every effort has been made to locate the authors or copyright holders of material in this anthology, and to give full and proper credit to each. We would be grateful to learn of any errors or omissions, which will be corrected in subsequent printings.

The editor wishes to thank the following for permission to reprint material:

Atsainak Akeeshoo, the Author and Frobisher Press, Ltd., for *Christmas in Hunting Camp;* Leah d'Argencourt, the Author, for *Christmas at Aulatsivik;* E. P. Dutton, Inc., for *That First Christmas Day in Baffin Island,* © 1956 by Elizabeth L. Fleming; Richard Finnie, the Author, for *Arctic Christmas;* Margery Hinds, the Author, for *Operation Santa Claus;* Harold Matson, Inc., Agent for the Author, for *A Little Drink to Fortify Himself,* © 1960 by Peter Freuchen; Howard Moorepark, Agent for the Author, for *Warmth Beneath the Snow;* Minister of Supply and Services, Canada, for *Christmas Time in Northern Labrador,* from *Inuktitut* magazine; and for *The Feast of Sedna, Eskimo Christmas Tree, Christmas in the Big Igloo, Community Christmas,* and *Quviasukvik — The Time for Rejoicing,* all from *north/nord* magazine; University of Saskatchewan Press, the Publisher, for *Christmas in the Wilderness.*

See also Sources on pages 53 and 54 of this book.

Contents

Introduction

"A horrible mockery of the spirit of Christmas," wrote Charles Edward Smith in 1866, to describe the deprivation faced by the crew of a whaler locked in the ice off Canada's Arctic coast. Yet George Francis Lyon, an earlier Northern explorer, had written of "good humour and merriment on a Christmas Day." These are two extreme views of the Christmas season in the Far North.

In popular image the Arctic is a bleak, inhospitable wasteland where winter temperatures plunge to impossible depths in a land vast and forbidding, ringed by frozen seas, swept always by relentless wind. But this is only one face of the Arctic, for the North has been many things to the diverse peoples who have called it home. To the Inuit, whose true home it is, the Arctic provides expanses of land and sea which are also the habitat of myriad animal resources on which their survival has depended for centuries. To the white man, the North has usually been something quite different than to the Inuit, although paradoxically it has not held the same attractions for all whites.

The Arctic of today has changed considerably from the remote Arctic of the early whalers and explorers. It has changed, too, from the isolated Arctic of the missionaries, traders and police. Arctic communities today are modern, well-serviced towns and villages with satellite communications networks and regular air transport. And it is not only the whites in the North who feel these changes; the North has changed for the Inuit as well. Christianity has long since supplanted traditional religious values. The snowmobile has virtually replaced the dogteam. Prefabricated wooden dwellings have taken the place of snowhouses and skin tents. Television and radio have made the Inuit an informed part of the world community.

Inuit and the various waves of whites who have come North have shared many aspects of Northern life. They have shared isolation, the cold and dark of interminable winters, and the unbounded joy of the brief burst of summer, whose endless days make unthinkable the impending darkness of yet another winter. And, if they are fortunate, they have shared Christmas.

The farther north one travels, the darker becomes midwinter. Christmas comes in the middle of this time, in the depth of winter's gloom. Before the coming of missionaries, many Canadian Inuit observed a midwinter ceremony which corresponded roughly in time to the celebration of the Europeans' Christmas. It is as if, psychologically, a celebration was needed in this darkest period of winter to break the monotony and to give people, regardless of their culture, a sense of renewal while awaiting the return of light and warmth.

Many whites have written of their experiences in the Canadian Arctic. There are books and articles by explorers, whalers, missionaries, police officers, scientists, naturalists, civil servants, traders, teachers, housewives and journalists. Many of these have written, in passing, of Christmas. It was something they held in common, an observance in which all, despite their differences, could share.

In recent years Inuit too have written accounts of Christmas in the North, the festive season as experienced by people who are not isolated from friends and relatives but at home in their Northern environment.

This book draws together selections describing Christmas in the Arctic over the past two hundred years. Each selection describes a separate Christmas in the long chain of Arctic winters. Each is in its own way special, whether it tells of harrowing cold, illness and starvation; of isolation made more bleak by memories of other feast days and kindlier winters; or of the simple joy of inner warmth contrasting with the cold outside. Together, these writings truly evoke the spirit of Christmas in the Canadian Arctic.

Kenn Harper
Arctic Bay
Northwest Territories
1983

ALLERTON

Christmas at Winter Harbour

William Edward Parry

William Edward Parry was the first of many British explorers to winter in the High Arctic in the course of the search for a Northwest Passage. Parry, in command of the Hecla, *wintered at Melville Island in the High Arctic in the winter of 1819-20. The* Hecla, *in company with its sister ship, the* Griper, *was completely isolated – not even Inuit lived that far north. To keep morale high in the dark of winter, Parry established a theatre of sorts on board ship, as well as a weekly newspaper which he called the* North Georgia Gazette and Winter Chronicle. *On later voyages he would also establish schools in which officers would instruct seamen in reading, writing and spelling. Parry spent four Christmases in the Arctic; his first, in the anchorage he named Winter Harbour, is described in his journal with the businesslike dispatch befitting an English officer.*

On Christmas Day the weather was raw and cold, with a considerable snow-drift, though the wind was only moderate from the N.W.; but the snow which falls during the severe winter of this climate is composed of spiculae so extremely minute, that it requires very little wind to raise and carry it along. To mark the day in the best manner which circumstances would permit, divine service was performed on board the ships; and I directed a small increase in the men's usual proportion of fresh meat as a Christmas dinner, as well as an additional allowance of grog, to drink the health of their friends in England. The officers also met at a social and friendly dinner, and the day passed with much of the same kind of festivity by which it is usually distinguished at home; and, to the credit of the men be it spoken, without any of that disorder by which it is too often observed by seamen.

1

Good Humour and Merriment on a Christmas Day

George Francis Lyon

In 1821 William Edward Parry in the Fury *and George Francis Lyon in command of the* Hecla *were dispatched by the British Admiralty on an expedition to search for a passage along the west coast of Foxe Basin north from Repulse Bay. The ships passed the next two winters in Foxe Basin. The Englishmen celebrated their first Christmas among themselves – no Inuit had yet been encountered. Lyon was an extremely observant officer and his skilfull writing provided more careful and colourful descriptions of the Arctic than had Parry's. He left the description which follows of the Christmas of 1821 at Winter Island, near Igloolik.*

December 22nd, our shortest day, was extremely fine, and the sun rose to 37° above the horizon, giving us three hours daylight, at least sufficiently clear to allow of our taking a long walk. How great the difference between this place and Melville Island, where, for ninety days, the sun was not seen! Comfortless as an Arctic winter certainly is, yet it has degrees of wretchedness, amongst which the absence of light is the most severely felt. This winter, however, we were blessed by the daily appearance of the sun, although it was powerless as to warmth.

On Christmas Eve, in order to keep the people quiet and sober, we performed two farces, and exhibited phantasmagoria, so that the night passed merrily away.

Christmas Day was very fine, and we all attended church on board the *Fury*, as we had been accustomed to do every Sunday since we were frozen in. The people then returned to their dinners, at which English roast beef, that had been kept untainted since the transport left us, was the principal luxury. To this were added cranberry pies and puddings of every shape and size, with full allowance of spirits. I never indeed saw more general good humour and merriment on a Christmas Day since I went to sea. A pretty compliment was paid to all the officers by a well meaning, but certainly not very sober crew, by absolutely forcing each in his turn, beginning with myself, to go out on the lower deck, and have his health drank with three hearty cheers.

On the 26th, we sent all the people for a run on the ice, in order to put them to rights, but thick weather coming on, it became necessary to recall them, and, postponing the dinner hour, they were all danced sober by 1 P.M., the fiddler being, fortunately, quite as he should be. During this curious ball, a witty fellow attended as an old cake woman, with lumps of frozen snow in a bucket; and such was the demand for his pies on this occasion, that he was obliged to replenish pretty frequently. At night we were all much startled by an account of a bear being seen between the ships, and arms were prepared, but the return of daylight gave us no traces of him.

3

We Kept Christmas Well and Long

Otto Sverdrup

The Norwegian Arctic expedition under the command of Otto Sverdrup passed four consecutive winters in Ellesmere Island from 1898 to 1902. The purpose of Sverdrup's trip was exploration and its results were impressive – the expedition made extensive geographical discoveries in the High Arctic, especially in the island group which today bears Sverdrup's name. Sverdrup carried on an Arctic wintering tradition which had been initiated by British explorers in the Far North – the establishment of an occasional winter newspaper to entertain the crew.

As a Scandinavian, Sverdrup kept not only Christmas Eve and Christmas Day but the entire season, extending into early January. The festivities and merriment lightened the burden of the dark winter away from home and loved ones. Sverdrup has left eloquent descriptions of his four Christmases aboard his ship, the Fram; *two are reproduced here.*

Christmas 1898: Cape Sabine

The central point in our holiday-making was naturally Christmas, and then the *Fram* shone like a bride. She was scrubbed from floor to ceiling, her lamps were polished, flags and pennons floated from unexpected places, and Japanese lanterns shed upon us their softened light. Every man appeared in holiday attire and spirits, and what good cheer the vessel could produce was on the board and in the cups.

When the Christmas tree was brought in, everybody was quite silent for a moment – and then the merriment broke loose in earnest. As it stood there, with its glittering gold and silver tinsel, and its red and white candles, in the midst of our darkness here, it seemed to be a greeting from home and from above. It seemed as if we were being told that there was still life,

and that the light was not really gone. We thought that we were sitting amid our dear ones, could take them by the hand, could feel that they really lived; it was as if happy thoughts had been sent to us – and then we had to shout for joy and make a horrible noise, much worse than our four-footed friends outside in the snow. And what was a sob within us found expression in a terrible hubbub, especially when all the Christmas presents were undone. They were chiefly children's toys – for men who felt like children! Drums, trumpets, fireworks, dolls, Noah's arks, sneezing-powder, scratching-powder, marzipan pigs, and things of the kind. There was merriment beyond compare, and practical jokes without end.

Then came the mental part of the festivity. Assisted by the wittiest of the expedition as contributors, the doctor had started a paper, the *Friendly One*, named after the leader in Baumann's team, of which the first number was read aloud that evening.

The wit and sarcasm of the *Friendly One* resulted in the publication of a rival paper, the *Arctic Fox*, which appeared on New Year's Day, but was withdrawn the same evening for want of subscribers; and therewith ended our journalistic efforts on board the *Fram* for that winter.

When our Christmas gaiety had reached its height, we concluded the festivity with a dance, which was quite the proper thing for young people like ourselves. So, to the entrancing melodies of a musical-box, the otherwise so serious *Fram* folk danced with vigour, while the steward from the sofa made an eloquent speech on his favourite topics, love and food, which nobody had time to listen to.

We kept Christmas until January 3, when we settled down again to our work in the two cabins and 'tween decks.

Christmas 1899: Harbour Fiord

Christmas was rapidly approaching, and there was much to be done. Busy as we had been before, we were now still more so, and every day that passed made things worse. There were those on board who nevertheless sacrificed some of their valuable time making Christmas presents to give their companions pleasure.

A general cleaning of all the cabins and galley had to take place; there were clothes to be washed, and cakes made. The steward was still ill, suffering great pain, and there seemed no chance of his being up for some time to come. The responsible task of making Christmas cakes, Hassel would on no account take upon himself, so Schei and I had to gather courage and do the best we could: nobody could ask more. We arranged matters so that Hassel had the galley to himself during the daytime, and we made havoc there at night.

The first night we made what promised to be the most delicious pastry. As all experts know, this is a lengthy business, and we were the whole night about it, if I except certain preparatory steps concerning the Christmas punch which we had to boil ourselves, likewise at dead of night.

Next evening, when all was silent, we began again on our baking exploits. But, to our horror, we found the pastry frozen! There it lay, as hard and cold as a lump of polar ice. This was a pretty business. However, there was nothing for it but to try and thaw our handiwork, of which before we had been so proud. This operation proved to be a dangerous one, for if we were not very careful the butter trickled out again. Our hopes of a successful baking sank in a disquieting degree; and they sank still lower when Schei, who had been intently studying the cookery-book, read out, in a trembling voice: *Pastry must not be exposed to a temperature so low that it will freeze.* There, then, was our fate, sealed in clear incontrovertible terms!

At this stage of the proceedings we began to rack our brains to know what in the world we were to do with all this beautiful pastry, if it was no use baking it in Christian fashion; but, try as we would, we could find no solution to the problem. At last in desperation we resolved to take our chance, and, at any rate, bake some small cakes.

Consumed with anxiety, we fell to work, and watched the course of events, prepared for the worst. It was a long time before we ventured to look into the oven; but at last we cautiously opened the door, and, putting our heads together, peeped in. Schei had on his glasses, and certainly this time they were not dim from moisture.

Things inside looked much better than we had dared to hope. The wretched little bits of pastry that we had put in had risen to miniature balloons. We drew a sigh of relief and went on with courage to greater undertakings; and before Hassel came in in the morning and drove us out we had the satisfaction of seeing the whole big lump of pastry transformed into the most beautiful cakes.

Christmas Eve this year fell on a Sunday. At twelve o'clock we had a dram by way of accompaniment. Afterwards both the cabins were decorated with flags and pennons, and, dressed in our best, we all – that is to say, all who were on their legs – assembled at a five o'clock dinner.

Out of consideration for our new steward, the bill of fare was this time rather simpler than usual. It consisted of *fiskegratin*, a baked compound of fish-flour, eggs, and butter; saddle-of-beef, green peas, asparagus, stewed cloudberries and rice, followed by coffee, curacao and cakes, and finally by the punch-bowl.

This year also each man had presents, some of which had been brought with us from friends at home. Like last year, they consisted chiefly of children's toys. The evening passed off as cheerfully as we could in any way expect. Our spirits were good, and the conversation was unflagging until late in the evening. Some songs were sung, and Isachsen played on his violin.

According to our good old Norwegian custom, we were called on Christmas morning with coffee and cakes, to which was also added a dram. The serving of it was seen to by the steward, with Fosheim as his assistant.

Hard as we had worked all through the autumn and winter, up to the present time, Christmas bid fair to be no less of an exertion as far as most of us were concerned, though in quite another way. We set to work to overeat ourselves in true Norwegian fashion. The one who suffered most, however, was our young steward, on account of the many courses he had to dish up for breakfast, dinner, and supper. Of course he could overeat himself on Christmas Day, just as much as the rest of us, but while we were taking a well-earned after-dinner nap he had to stand out in the galley and wash up.

Simmons, poor fellow, was lying ill all this time with fever and headache; so, in order not to disturb him, we moved, when supper was over, to the after-cabin, there to enjoy songs and music, and the delicious but insidious bowl concocted by Baumann. The recipe alone was sufficiently promising – champagne, brandy, sugar, water, and fruit juice – and the result quite fulfilled the promise. Our thoughts at this time were chiefly fixed on keeping Christmas as well as possible; while Baumann's birthday, four days later, was a reason the more to keep the ball rolling.

On January 4 we gave up keeping Christmas, and went back to work again. . .

A Horrible Mockery of the Spirit of Christmas

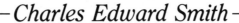 *Charles Edward Smith*

In the middle of the last century, whaling ships from Scotland and England frequented the waters of Davis Strait. Life aboard a whaling ship in the Arctic was harsh. On those voyages during which the vessel wintered in the North, the hardships were especially severe.

The Diana *was a well-known Arctic whaler in the mid-nineteenth century. In February of 1866 she left Hull, England, and, after sealing near Jan Mayen Island, rounded Cape Farewell and made for Baffin Bay for whales. After making Melville Bay, she crossed to Pond Inlet on the Baffin coast. In late September, southbound off Clyde River, she encountered solid pack ice. It was impenetrable. Rather than winter in Baffin Island, Captain John Gravill decided to run the* Diana *into the pack and drift with it into the Atlantic. Locked in the ice, the* Diana *drifted steadily southward close to the Baffin coast but, instead of being released into the Atlantic, the ice which carried her drifted up Frobisher Bay, running back and forth in the inlet with the tides and wind. On March 17, 1867, the ship was finally released from the pack and reached Lerwick in the Orkney Islands on April 11 with eight corpses on deck.*

The crew of the Diana *passed Christmas imprisoned in the ice of Frobisher Bay. It was a sombre and cheerless day. Captain Gravill was on his deathbed, attended by the surgeon, Charles Edward Smith, who left an account of the voyage.*

Tuesday, December 25th (Christmas Day) – I spent the entire night with the captain, who was extremely restless and uneasy. The weather during the night was horribly cold in the cabin.

At 8 A.M. I went on deck, and found the ship driving with great rapidity towards a large iceberg. We passed within three or four ship's lengths of the berg. We were most wonderfully preserved from driving upon it or being crushed by the whirling, crashing ice, which was in commotion far and wide around the berg, which is aground.

This morning the men held a prayer meeting in the half-deck, and, it being Christmas Day, they commenced with singing the chant, *How beautiful upon the mountains.*

Flour and plums having been served out yesterday, Joe, the cook, was up at three o'clock this morning, busy as a bee making plum puddings for the different messes. Every man and boy on board had a large slice of very good plum pudding served out to him at twelve o'clock in honour of Christmas Day. As most of the men have been saving up meat, biscuits, etc., you may be sure every one of our ship's company enjoyed a good dinner. In the cabin we dined at one o'clock, and had a large plum pudding, which was equally divided, our usual three quarters of a pound of boiled salt beef, and a dish of tripe. George Clarke, the mate, had brought this, pickled in a jar, from home, and it turned out to be fearfully salt.

ALLERSTON

We ate our Christmas dinner almost in silence, each man's mind being occupied with gloomy thoughts of home, families, and friends. The poor old dying captain lay upon the sofa, occasionally turning over or dozing uneasily in a half-unconscious slumber.

What a Christmas dinner! What thoughts of the many merry ones at Sandon, and at home, and of last year's Christmas at Mr Moffat's. What a change! Thoughts of father, brothers, and sisters, at home on Christmas Day, and thinking of *me*, as I am thinking of them.

To these thoughts add my anxieties and apprehensions on the captain's account, and the gloomy prospect before every one of us. You will readily believe that a more miserable Christmas dinner would be difficult to imagine even. The dinner, such as it was, was soon dispatched, and I was glad when 'twas over, it seemed such a horrible mockery of the spirit of an English Christmas.

At about 3 P.M. the ice was in motion again, and pressing heavily upon the ship. I happened to be on deck at the time, but instantly ran down to the cabin. Here I found the captain, whom I had left calm and tranquil and breathing regularly, changed for the worse in a sudden and alarming manner.

He had heard or felt the ship move under the pressure of the ice, and knew very well what it meant. He knew that the ship was in danger. He knew, whatever poor chance his ship's company had of saving their lives, *he* had none if the ship were stove in and we had to take to the ice.

Happily the pressure moderated and the ice became quieter. At 6 P.M. the captain was calmer, but evidently very much weaker, and more incoherent and difficult to understand.

Christmas in the High Arctic

Joseph-Elzear Bernier

Between 1906 and 1911 Joseph-Elzear Bernier, a veteran French-Canadian seaman from L'Islet, Quebec, made three official voyages to the Canadian High Arctic. On these he took possession of a vast reach of Arctic territory in the name of Canada. Two of his fondest dreams, to reach the North Pole and to navigate the Northwest Passage, were never to be fulfilled, yet fueling both those objectives was the desire to establish and to extend Canada's sovereignty over the Far North, and in this he succeeded admirably.

Before Bernier's time only one official Canadian government expedition had visited northern Baffin Island. The region was the domain of American and Scandinavian explorers and Scottish whalers. Bernier's real accomplishment was not in discovering new lands, but in securing Canada's claim to lands previously discovered and cursorily explored by a number of expeditions, largely British. He charted in more detail, described more accurately, and explored with more tenacity areas that had been found by others, and in so doing he secured forever his country's sovereignty in the High Arctic.

On each of his three voyages Bernier wintered, once on remote Melville Island, but twice in areas of northern Baffin Island where Inuit lived. He left detailed accounts of his winterings which include descriptions of how Christmas was passed at each location. What follows are Bernier's accounts of Christmas in 1906 at Albert Harbour, just west of the present-day community of Pond Inlet, and at Arctic Bay four years later.

Christmas 1906: Albert Harbour, Baffin Island

Saturday, *December 22nd* – Wind west. Weather clear and cold. At ten o'clock in the forenoon it is still too dark outside to permit us to read ordinary type; it is almost eleven o'clock in the forenoon before it is bright enough to read outside, and at one o'clock in the afternoon it is again too dark outside to read ordinary type. This will give an idea of the length of daylight there is this day. I invited the men to arrange and decorate their cabins for Christmas. A large hole about two hundred feet opened today in the ice, in the passage between the island and Baffin Land which was caused by the rush of water in this narrow passage. We had to put lines all around that hole, to prevent the men from falling in if they should happen to be around in the evening.

Monday, December 24th – General inspection of the ship today; the main deck and cabin are perfectly clean; the living rooms and state rooms have been properly washed and cleaned, and the officers have their state rooms well decorated for Christmas; they have put up flags and family photos, and every one seems to be proud of his room. It is very pleasing for the members of the expedition and entices them to visit one another, which visits have the result of making time appear much shorter than otherwise. Our native Kanaka was instructed to tell the other natives that they were invited to spend Christmas day on board with their families. I gave orders to the steward to have dinner ready for about one hundred natives. Preparations were made to receive them; I also sent an invitation to Captain Mutch to celebrate Christmas with us.

December 25th, Christmas Day – There was Sunday service in the forenoon; it was well attended by the members of the expedition and some of the natives who had already arrived for the dinner. At 1 P.M. all the natives had arrived on board with their families; about one hundred and twenty persons, they sat down to a good Canadian dinner. After dinner I addressed them a few words; telling them again that they were Canadians and would be treated as such as long as they would do what was right. At 7 P.M. tea and coffee were served to all the invited, and some candy was given to the children. A deputation of natives and some members of the crew came and asked my permission to dance on board. Knowing the pleasure it would afford them, I could not refuse the request and was glad to accede to their wishes and to see that they would amuse themselves. The natives behaved very well and there were no disturbances of any sort, but perfect good order reigned throughout. During the evening there were different tricks and acts done by the members of the expedition and natives. There were wrestling matches between Canadians and other matches of the same style between Eskimos; the men also performed acrobatic feats, juggling and other acts. Music selections from the pianola and the graphophone were given during the evening. The Eskimos danced to the music of the accordion. It was well on to twelve o'clock before the dance ceased and the natives left for their homes. Everybody seemed to have enjoyed himself immensely and was glad of the celebration.

Christmas 1910: Arctic Bay, Baffin Island

As Christmas was approaching an invitation was given Chief Nasso to take dinner on board the *Arctic,* by way of impressing him with the hospitality that the Captain was willing to extend to the native tribes. One remarkable incident in connection with some changes in the colour of the sky at the horizon, was the purple tint now observed, encouraging the men to look forward to the reappearance of the sun, with the advantages of daylight in exploring the surrounding country and making expeditions west and south. At this time some natives with their families from Fury and Hecla Strait and Agoo arrived on board the ship.

Christmas Day was fine and calm and all preparations for celebrating the day were completed. Forty natives from the Eskimo village, including those from Fury and Hecla Strait and Agoo, went on board the ship and amused and interested themselves, in various ways. Some of them attended the religious service which formed part of the day's engagements. Although silent and well-behaved, they seemed to be endeavouring to comprehend the meaning of the service and its purpose. Others of the natives roamed about the ship asking questions of those of the crew who did not attend the religious service, about each article that they did not know the use of nor value. A temporary table of some planed boards was arranged at which the natives sat down and food in sufficient quantity and of a kind to satisfy their simple tastes was served. They ate their Christmas dinner with relish and seemed, in their love for those things that appeal to hungry people accustomed to live on raw fish or flesh, to regret that "Christmas comes but once a year."

Some of the attention given the natives in this occasional hospitality had in view the object of teaching them that the Canadian Government was interested in their welfare, to give them some idea of the friendly spirit and to convey some knowledge of the treatment that they might expect, from the employees of the Canadian Government in accordance with British traditions, following the practice of explorers sent out by the Admiralty.

We Did Not Pass a Very Merry Christmas

Alfred Tremblay

In 1911, after the conclusion of his third expedition to the High Arctic, Captain Bernier retired from government service to become a private trader. The following year, his tiny schooner, the Minnie Maud, *sailed north to Pond Inlet with Bernier and his crew to prospect for gold and to trade for furs and ivory with the Inuit. The party wintered at Albert Harbour. Alfred Tremblay, a young French-Canadian prospector, was part of that expedition. It was his second trip to the North. On Bernier's previous expedition, Tremblay and his friend and fellow prospector, Arthur English, had discovered the ore body on Strathcona Sound which is now the Nanisivik Mine.*

During the winter of 1912-13 Tremblay travelled extensively in northern Baffin Island, and passed a cheerless Christmas at Arctic Bay.

Just before Christmas our stock of provisions was exhausted, as also our stock of gasoline. We did not pass a very merry Christmas; our Christmas dinner consisted of a little flour and grease that we cooked in a frying pan over a kerosene lamp. After that, we borrowed some seal meat and blubber from Etotah, at Strathcona Sound, who, fortunately, could spare us a little. We were beginning to get very anxious when some more provisions arrived from Pond Inlet on December 30th which were brought by Attita and Nooyeeso. The small shack leaked badly as the snow and frost on the walls and roofs kept condensing from the heat of the lamp and the gasoline stove, and bedding and clothing were continuously damp from the drippings of the roof. We got our drinking and cooking water, which was of the best, from the lake, in the surface of which we cut a large hole and which we kept from freezing over by packing with snow. We built a snow igloo over the water hole to protect it from the dogs.

We did not see the sun for nearly three months, until the 5th of February, and the days were long, dark and depressing. At Christmas especially, we felt as if we were abandoned on the frozen rim of the world. Inside the shack was dirt, gloom, discomfort, and irksome inaction; while outside was nothing but bleak, black rocks, snow and ice-covered desolation, wrapped in dense fog and accompanied by an intense, biting cold that would not allow itself for one moment to be forgotten. The north wind howled round the shack in bitter blasts, often accompanied by whirling blizzards of snow. To add to our discomfort we were uncertain whether our provisions would be able to reach us from Pond Inlet in time, as the long silence which had ensued since the requisition which we had sent was making us very uneasy.

Christmas in the Wilderness

Bernhard Adolph Hantzsch

Bernhard Adolph Hantzsch was a scientist and explorer who passed the Christmas of 1910 in surroundings quite different from those of Bernier and his crew, hundreds of miles north in Arctic Bay. Hantzsch, isolated by choice from other white men, endured a hard Christmas with a small band of Inuit on the shores of Foxe Basin. It was his last Christmas anywhere.

Hantzsch was a German ornithologist who had come out to Cumberland Sound in 1909 aboard a whaling ship. The ship, the Jantina Agatha, *was wrecked and sunk in the sound; her crew and passengers reached Blacklead Island in the ship's boats, unharmed but having lost most of their supplies. Hantzsch passed the winter in cramped quarters at the whaling station at Blacklead and the following spring set out via Nettilling Lake for the unexplored coast of Foxe Basin. Travelling with the Inuit, he shared their food and their clothing, but not their temperament nor their resigned attitude to hardship. Several times the party was near starvation. In the spring of 1911, the party killed a polar bear; it saved Hantzsch from starvation, but transmitted to him the means of a more lingering death, the dreaded germs of trichinosis, borne in the flesh of the bear.*

Hantzsch died on the shores of Foxe Basin at the end of May, 1911. His journal, written in German, was taken back to Blacklead Island by the Inuit and entrusted to the Reverend Greenshield. Translated by Leslie H. Neatby, it was published in 1977 by the University of Saskatchewan under the title My Life Among the Eskimos. *In it Hantzsch describes Christmas of 1910 at his camp in Foxe Basin.*

Saturday, 24 December – Holy Christmas Eve! I am finishing a letter begun yesterday to my people at home, and then continue with my writing. The weather is so bad (wind and drift) that my people stay indoors where it is warm and comfortable. Ittusakdjuak has made a little humming-top with which he, Sirkinirk and Aggulukdjuk amuse themselves for hours on end.

Sunday, 25 December – Christmas in the wilderness! I have a talk with Ittusakdjuak early in the morning before he goes out and tell him that I do not enjoy being governed by a woman. Sirkinirk's overbearing manner annoys me. So we quickly come to an understanding and I produce my little gifts: Ittusakdjuak – two pocket knives, one shirt, one piece of tobacco; Sirkinirk – one shirt, red cloth and thread, one dishcloth, one third piece of tobacco; Aggakdjuk – one pair under trousers, one pocket knife, one piece of tobacco; Arnga – material, thread, washcloth, one third piece of tobacco; Aggulukdjuk – one pocket knife, one third piece of tobacco. Then I produce the Christmas cookery: fine meal biscuit, three quarter meal, one soup tablet (potato), some salt, one tin of milk in warm water, one-half pound of fresh-cut apple-fritters, thirty-two little biscuits cooked with fat in a tin over the blubber lamp, five raisins in each. Then cocoa is brewed. Aggakdjuk, Ittusakdjuak and I myself, each one of the last tins of milk. And then for the biscuits. A splendidly successful and fitting end to the day. Ittusakdjuak gives me a thick caribou skin, the only one of those left behind which the fox spared out of which Sirkinirk will make me stockings and other things for the spring journey. Sirkinirk has sewn me a pretty little *Tischchen* (table cover) out of the skin of caribou legs.

Aggakdjuk does not come, and it is so dark, that I will not visit him in his own house, but will keep the little gifts for the next day. It is nearly ten o'clock when well fed and contented we go to bed.

Monday, 26 December – Bitter cold, and a light wind from the north/northeast, but my people go out to their work at daybreak (nine-thirty). It is truly a cold task to remain standing over a breathing hole, but our meat is all spent, though so far Aggak-djuk has kept us sufficiently supplied, but after their period of hunger his family will not have much left of their seal, but some food remains for the dogs, and, if the worst comes to the worst, we will be back to soup tablets in a few days, in order to preserve a little food for the dogs. Yesterday Aggulukdjuk saw a seal in the water and each of my people knows of a breathing hole that is still being used, so that, sooner or later, a seal will be killed. I will not get much work done on this holiday, for petty odd jobs are so troublesome that they rob me of much time. Actually I do hardly any writing, for I must again put my

boxes in order. I bring my little gifts over to Arnga, who seems much pleased, and invites me to stay for a while. She is always courteous and modest, at least in my presence, and is the only one of my women with whom I have not yet had a set-to. As the daughter of a European she feels that she has some affinity to my ways. I tell her something of my troubles with Sirkinirk and amuse myself with the infant which now has eight teeth (four plus four), but still lives almost exclusively at his mother's breast.

Aggakdjuk has been watching the open water with Aggulukdjuk and after the latter departed he comes home with nothing but a well-shot-up *Cepphus* (seabird). Aggulukdjuk vainly pursues a hare; Ittusakdjuak watches a breathing hole until dusk with equal ill-success. Aggakdjuk brings over to me a weasel carved out of a walrus tusk; he had no other material to work on. In the evening a regular Christmas meal, somewhat upset by a visit by two children and Aggulukdjuk, and so slightly less pleasant than that of the day before.

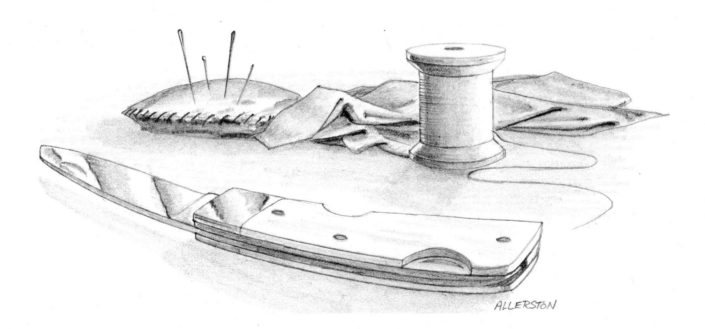

ALLERSTON

15

That First Christmas Day in Baffin Land

Archibald Lang Fleming

It was not until 1894 that the first resident missionary, Edmund James Peck, arrived in Baffin Island to minister to the Inuit from the mission he established at Blacklead Island in Cumberland Sound.

In 1913 Archibald Lang Fleming went as missionary to the tiny community of Lake Harbour on the south shore of Baffin Island. There, with the help of Julian Bilby, an experienced Arctic missionary, he worked with the Inuit of Hudson Strait. Many years later Fleming became Bishop of the Arctic. He described his first Christmas in Baffin Island when he published his memoirs under the title Archibald the Arctic.

Our time was so taken up that before we knew it Christmas had arrived. The dawn of that first Christmas Day in Baffin Land was calm and still. We were disappointed that the sun did not show itself but the sky was completely overcast and low misty clouds could be seen hurrying westward. By eleven o'clock a strong north wind was driving the snow before it, causing a peculiar rustling noise as it swirled around the house.

It had been agreed that on this great day the house would be kept warm and that for the first time since the whaler had left us we would dress in civilized apparel. It gave me a strange feeling to enjoy the luxury of a white shirt, linen collar, fine socks, and leather shoes.

The day began with our Christmas service in English but as we were two only I fear our thoughts wandered to the South with its crowded churches, carols, and bells.

When worship was over Bilby said that, since he was cook, he wanted the kitchen to himself. I retired to my room for nearly two hours, spent first in private devotion, and then I had a glorious time reading Christmas letters and opening presents.

Perhaps I should explain that, at the suggestion of Peck, I had asked my friends to date all letters and parcels on the outside and I had promised that I would keep them unopened until that particular date twelve months hence. In this way I had the joy of receiving letters and parcels throughout the year, even when I was away from the mission house and living with the Eskimo.

Although relieved of all cooking responsibilities, I was allotted the task of "table maid" while Yarley proved a most willing and helpful dishwasher. Bilby, to my great satisfaction, left the arrangement and decorations of the table entirely to me.

It was our everyday practice to have our meals in the dining room, never in the kitchen. Three times a day the red tablecloth was removed and replaced by a white cloth. On this occasion we had a really fine linen cloth on the table, and linen napkins replaced our ordinary cotton ones. A pair of small brass candlesticks, some artificial flowers made by the blind in Glasgow, an embroidered centerpiece, a specially designed menu card bound with a little blue silk ribbon, fruit and candy, gave a festive appearance to the table which surprised and greatly pleased even Bilby.

Yarley was dressed in "white man's" clothes, including a large apron of bleached cotton made especially for the occasion by an Eskimo woman. I had trimmed the lad's hair and let him plaster it down with some of my hair tonic.

The food was cooked to perfection, well served and seasoned. Here is what the menu cards said:

Seal Soup

Arctic Hare – Jugged

Arctic Ptarmigan – Baked

Caribou Steaks – Fried

Fresh Potatoes – from St. John's, Nfld.

Onion – Canned, from England

Plum Pudding – Canned, from England

Fruit – Canned, from England

Jelly – from England

Candies – from Canada

Coffee – from St. John's, Nfld.

We sat down to dinner at half past one o'clock and in an hour all was over! But what a happy time we had.

As soon as the house was once more set in order, we called the Eskimo to service and Bilby told them the story of Bethlehem. Never shall I forget the eager upturned faces and the look of joy and wonder written across the dusky features. From time to time, as was their happy way, the people indicated their pleasure, surprise, or approval by such expressions as *E* (Yes!), *E-la-le* (Certainly!) or *Ka-pay* (Wonderful!). As they listened, I prayed that the Saviour of the world might be born anew in the hearts of these dwellers in Arctic night.

After the service we invited our friends to a feast. Bilby had laboured diligently to provide the kind of food likely to be enjoyed by our guests. Two large steaming puddings something like our Christmas pudding but not nearly so rich were served with molasses for sauce. These were followed by quantities of thick currant scones fried in marrow fat, and steaming coffee. Gradually the feasting ended and each Eskimo in turn expressed thanks. It was then my privilege to play selections on our little Victor gramophone with its funny metal trumpet. Music always stirred the Eskimo to glowing enthusiasm but they had a hard time understanding the gramophone and wanted to know where I kept the little man in the Talking Box.

Before we parted we gave each of our visitors a present as another reminder that on Christmas Day we commemorated God's Great Gift to all "the inhabitants of the world" and that this was a free gift that could not be obtained by barter.

Many of these Christmas presents had been generously supplied by the Women's Auxiliary of the Church of England in Canada. Bilby and I contributed various items from our common store or some personal possessions which we felt would be of special value to particular Eskimo. After the distribution of gifts we sang a Christmas hymn and closed with a prayer of thanksgiving, the Christmas Collect, and the Benediction.

When the people had departed after much handshaking and many expressions of thanks, Bilby, Yarley, and I had a busy time washing up dishes and cleaning the house. Finally all was in order once more so Yarley returned to his family while Bilby drank tea with me in my room and enjoyed Scotch cake and shortbread. We then went to bed, each to think his own thoughts of past days and of loved ones.

The Feast of Sedna

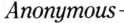 *Anonymous*

Before the coming of missionaries to the Arctic, the Inuit of course had their own beliefs and traditions. One of these involved a mid-winter ceremony which, by coincidence, occurred at about the same time of the year as the observance of Christmas. This tradition, now abandoned, was described in an article in north *in 1969.*

In the early days, the Eskimos had a great winter feast that they held at about the same time of the year as our Christmas. It was celebrated by most of the groups across the Arctic, with some variation in ritual from Alaska in the west to Cumberland Sound on east Baffin Island.

The central figure of the occasion was Sedna, evil mistress of the underworld. During the season of late autumn storms in the Cumberland Sound area, the most powerful Eskimo sorcerers would gather in a large hut. One would lure Sedna up from the ground with a magic song; two others would stand over the opening formed by a coil of rope on the floor. When Sedna rose through the hard rock, she was harpooned. She struggled to escape but the two men would hold with all their strength. Finally she broke away leaving them with the blood-sprinkled harpoon. This they proudly showed to the people.

On the following day of the feast, all the people wore amulets on the tops of their hoods, to protect them from the enraged and wounded goddess. The amulet was a part of the first garment which they wore after birth.

The festival began in the early morning, when all the men gathered and ran screaming and jumping around the houses. Then, in a group they visited every house; the women would come and throw out a dish holding bits of seal meat, ivory carvings or sealskin artifacts.

Then the crowd divided into two parties for a tug-of-war. If the "ptarmigans" (those who were born in the winter) lost to the "ducks" (those born in the summer), fine weather would be expected through the winter.

Next the women brought a large kettle of water into the centre of the gathering. The oldest man dipped out a cup of water, sprinkled a few drops on the ground, turned his face toward the land of his youth and spoke his name and the place of his birth. He was followed in this ritual by an older woman and then by all the others in turn.

Suddenly, two heavy masked figures, the *qailertetang*, appeared. The crowd screamed and shrank back from them. The *qailertetang* ceremoniously divided the men and women into rows, matched them in pairs, and pursued each pair to the house of the woman where they would live for the following day and night as man and wife.

The masked figures then strode to the shore and invoked the north wind, which brought good weather, and warned off the unfavourable south wind.

Christmas Time in Northern Labrador

Sam Metcalfe

In Labrador, Christmas celebrations extend into early January. The final event of the festive season is Nalujuk's Night *or* Jannies' Night. *Celebrated on January 6, it seems to be a blending of the pre-Christian Sedna ritual of the Inuit and the Christian observance of the twelve days of Christmas which ends on January 6, Three Kings' Day.* Nalujuk *is an Inuit word meaning "the one who is ignorant or uninformed." The English equivalent,* Jannies, *used by the settler population of Labrador, is of unknown origin. The tradition also bears resemblance to the Newfoundland practice of mummery, and is maintained to this day.*

Sam Metcalfe is an Inuk from Labrador who lives in Ottawa where he works in Inuit cultural and linguistic programs. He has taught the Inuktitut language at Ottawa University and at Memorial University. He wrote the article which follows for Inuktitut *magazine in 1978.*

Christmas time in Labrador, particularly in Hebron, was visibly centered on and around religion, according to my recollections of it when I was about seven years old.

The personality of everyone dramatically changed around that time, as well as at Easter. Those who were prone to drinking, fighting or arguing suddenly became kind, loving and attended all of the endless church services and completely ceased "unreligious" activities. There was peace and quiet, a hushed stillness like calm waters and clean air after a sudden storm, which lasted for some time. It had high peaks and less severe squalls while it lasted.

For endless weeks prior to Christmas, everybody was busy getting ready for the big events. (I say events because the season, religiously speaking, lasted for many weeks and had more than one highlight.)

The women were cleaning house, cooking food, washing and sewing new clothes for the whole household. The men were out cutting and fetching firewood by dog team on every fine day. The church elders went around getting men to cut wood for the church and other men were delegated to clean and paint the interior of the church before decorating it. Two trees with candles were put up in front. The doorways, window frames and walls were decorated with boughs while the posts, beams and trim were done up with red, white and blue paper streamers. It smelled like an evergreen forest and made you feel as if you were inside a cool greenhouse. At every eye contact with another, there were prolonged and affectionate smiles or words of praise and kindness on meeting. Surprisingly enough, none of these expressions seemed forced. It all seemed so spontaneous and natural.

All or most of the meat was caught and stored away ready for use. The caribou and seal meat was distributed to all those who could not afford, or were unable to get, their own.

The clotheslines were filled with various items of clothing, but what stood out the most were the newly washed or brand new white *silapaaks* (home-made cotton coats) swaying like armour in the wind. Each *silapaak* was trimmed with ribbons of blue, red, green or black around the edges, sleeves and hood. The *silapaaks* of the women were more decorative than those of the

men. They had beadwork on a black background around the hood and multi-coloured ribbon trimmings. A lot of them had highly valuable and intricately carved pieces of ivory hanging all around the entire lower edge of the *silapaak* or "dickie" (duffle parka).

There were also all kinds and sizes of skin boots hung out on wooden flakes, drying and getting a shine in the cold frosty air. Some of the skin boots were of the plain ordinary type, black tops and bottoms with the hair removed. Some had white bottoms and black tops with or without the hair. Some of the sealskin boots had various designs sewn on the front part of the leggings or tops. There were skin boots with no boot strings which had plain or fancy caribou skin trimmings around the top and some boots had any colour or a combination of colours of wool or cotton for boot strings, with or without wool tassels at the ends. (Of course, there were people who wore just an old army jacket or a pair of rubber boots by choice or because of necessity.)

At our house, when it was getting close to Christmas Eve, we were sent to bed earlier because Mom wanted to sew and make something to surprise us. Dad chipped and banged away at wood, making toys. I remember that one year he made a large wooden rocking horse which we had for a long time afterwards. Usually, we were so excited that we stayed awake half the night wondering what they were making for us. Our light bill must have climbed in those weeks because the kerosene lamps and the Aladdin lamps burned into the wee hours of the morning, not to mention the many armloads of wood and numerous chunks of coal and seal fat that went into the kitchen stove.

Christmas Eve finally came and we looked for the biggest woolen stocking we could find to hang up on a nail behind the stove, on the window sill or on a doorknob.

Christmas morning, we got up before daylight to look for our stockings, as the custom in our house was that Mom or Dad would hide the stockings and we would look everywhere for them. The idea was to find your own but not tell the others if you happened to find theirs. The stockings would contain evaporated slices of apples, dried apricots, raisins, prunes, candy and some item of clothing such as a new pair of skin boots or skin mitts.

It seemed there were church services every day for weeks. The church bell kept ringing and the brass band would play hymns at five or six o'clock in the morning throughout the whole village. Sometimes they would play again during the afternoon or late at night. There were six or seven musicians. All of their instruments were covered with duffle material, tailor-made to protect their hands from the cold. Other men would follow in order to relieve those who grew cold or tired. They always came into our house to get warm and have a rest, although it was more probably because Dad gave them pipe tobacco or chewing tobacco, and they were always asked to play a tune. I found it very pleasant to wake up to the sound of the brass band early in the morning. First the music was very faint, for they would start at a house which was at the far end of the village. As they made their way gradually through the village, the music became louder and louder, and we were fully awake by the time they got to our house. Some days, they would climb to the roof of the church or gather at the top of the steeple and play for hours. On clear days, the music was loud and echoed for miles. On windy days, we could hear only spurts of it unless we were very close to them.

On the day we saw people hauling water to the church, we knew there was going to be a "Love Feast." Water would be boiled in large pots on a pot-bellied stove in the church and, at the service, on cue from the Minister, the church Elders would get up and serve tea and biscuits. No one was left out. If there were not enough white enameled mugs to go around, the Elders would collect the empty mugs from the first rows and have them washed out. While the serving of tea and biscuits was going on, the congregation kept on singing hymns. Above the singing could be heard the clanking of metal cups on wooden trays.

On one side of the church, where all the females sat (males on the opposite side), there would be four or five rows of mothers with crying babies busily trying to hush them by breast-feeding, rocking side to side, or doing anything that worked. But the crying and the whining kept on throughout the service.

If the young boys or girls in the front rows misbehaved in any way, one of the Elders would get up and speak to them. If that didn't make them behave, they would be separated and if that also failed, they could even be thrown out of the church.

There were all kinds of special church services – young men's day, young women's day, married men's day, married women's day, widow's day, and widower's day. For boys and girls at Christmas time there was the Candlelight Service. At this service, we were given a bun, an apple or whatever else was available, with a lighted candle stuck into it. Only the babies and children were served this special treat. All of the lights were turned out, and the elders walked in with lighted candles carried on large wooden trays.

There was also a midnight service on New Year's Eve. Getting close to the midnight hour, the Minister would be reading from the Bible, all of the babies and a few of the adults would be fast asleep, and everything would be quiet. All of a sudden people would jump out of their seats with fright because at that precise moment there was an ear-shattering noise from the brass band, the organ, the stringed orchestra, the church bells and the guns, all going off together to welcome the New Year. It's a unique experience which I'll never forget. There's a story that a man in Nain died during such a service, probably from a combination of heart failure and fright.

The next special day was *Nalujuk* (Heathen) Day or Old Christmas Day which was January 6. The night before, we would go around to any number of houses, hanging up our stockings. Early the next morning, it was exciting to go back to collect our gifts. During the day, there were more church services. At one of them all the information about what had gone on during the past year was given out. It was an annual news report. You learned who was born, who died, who got married, who moved in from where and who moved out to where, and you learned of any other statistics that might or might not be of interest.

Sometime during the day, six or seven men would leave the village unnoticed by us. As it began to get dark, we would see them coming around the point, heading for the houses. They were dressed up in fur clothing and wore ugly-looking face masks. Even their hands were covered with something furry that served as a mitt. Each one carried a weapon of some sort, such as a harpoon, whip, stick or a piece of chain. Each one had a large bag hanging in front with a string around his neck. If anyone happened to be out of doors when they arrived, he was chased until he ran into a house. Hardly anyone escaped without first getting a hard whack across the bottom with a whip or a stick. The *Nalujuk* people went into every house. The older boys and men would gather outside and entice the *Nalujuk* to chase them. Those being chased tried to run to any house which had not been paid a visit and the *Nalujuks* would chase them into that house. When they entered a house they sought out the children and asked them or their parents if they had been good. If they had been bad during the year, they got a firm smack and were told not to be bad anymore. They were commanded to always listen to and respect older people, especially mothers and fathers. Each child had to sing a song or recite a poem. If any children refused to do so, they were given a smack and not left alone until they cried. If they sang or recited, they were rewarded. After the *Nalujuk* had listened, they would reach into their bags and give out goodies, which could be anything from candies to prunes to home-made toys or clothing. Some of the parents prearranged with a *Nalujuk* to give a certain child something extra good.

The next day the trees and decorations were taken down and life once more returned to normal. The people went back to hunting, working, dancing and some went back to drinking or whatever they chose to do.

Everything in a small village, whether it be the good things or the bad, seems to be much more noticeable than it is in large cities. You have to try to please everybody all of the time. In a large city, you can avoid certain people if you happen to dislike them in any way. But in a small village there is no getting away from anyone or anything, not even religion and the *Nalujuk*.

23

A Little Drink to Fortify Himself

Peter Freuchen

In 1921 Knud Rasmussen, Greenlandic ethnographer and explorer, launched a major scientific expedition to the Canadian Arctic, his Fifth Thule Expedition. Accompanying him was his long-time friend and fellow scientist, Peter Freuchen. A giant of a man, Freuchen was a keen observer of his surroundings and a shrewd judge of the people he met in the Arctic. He left a wealth of information, mixed with humorous and skilfully told anecdotes, in the many books he published before his death in 1957. One of the many intriguing characters he met in the Keewatin during the Fifth Thule Expedition was a white man, a former whaler named George Washington Cleveland. Cleveland figured prominently in the Christmas Freuchen passed at Repulse Bay.

Captain Cleveland – Sakoatarnak – was quite a person and not without merit. He lived there, the only white man, and his word was law over a district larger than many states in the United States.

Cleveland was a great character. When we asked him, during our first meal together, whether he would object to our bringing out a bottle of our famous Danish *schnapps* he assured us that we could make ourselves at home in his house as long as we desired. "In fact," he assured us, "liquor is my favorite drink – any kind and any brand."

He was limited to six bottles a year "for medical purposes." But, as he was usually ill the very day after the ship arrived with the year's supply, he almost never had any left over for subsequent illnesses.

Captain Cleveland boasted of his cooking and said that he would prepare a Christmas dinner of eight courses, no more and no less. At two o'clock he would start to work, but to gather physical strength and morale for the ordeal he would first have a drink or two. He gulped them down, and we listened to some of his stories. When it was lunchtime he asked me to prepare it, as he would need all his strength and enthusiasm for the dinner. He was going to cook us a dinner of five courses, no more, no less, just to show us that one of the best cooks in the world lived at Repulse Bay.

But he needed a little drink to fortify himself. And after some moments he said that he was about to prepare us a dinner, a *real* Christmas dinner, of four courses, no more, no less. But surely a man deserved a drink before he commenced work.

He was almost stiff after that, but the three-course dinner he was about to prepare would be better than anything we had ever tasted – especially as he was to serve us caribou roast. First, of course, it would have to thaw out, and while it thawed he would occupy his time with a little drink. Unfortunately he took the drink first, and the caribou meat remained outside in a temperature of forty below.

By this time the rest of us were ravenous. Captain Berthie, who had come up for Christmas, volunteered to cook the dinner himself, but Cleveland vetoed the idea. No, sir, he would cook us a real Northern Christmas dinner. He knew that we did not believe in many courses, nor did he. There would be just one course, but it would be caribou roast like nothing we had ever tasted.

It was rather difficult for him to stand now, but he asked me to help him, and I got him into the kitchen where we discovered, much to our amazement, that the meat had not come in by itself. It was still outside frozen hard as a rock, but Cleveland said, "To hell with it; we'll put it in the oven and let it thaw out while it roasts."

Cleveland proceeded with his incredible yarns, but was interrupted by the odour of something burning. We rushed out and found the kitchen full of smoke. It was, however, only the meat roasting as it thawed.

He and I now proceeded with the meal. Cleveland was actually a fine cook. Quickly he took the meat from the oven and carved away the burnt portions. By now the interior was thawed out and ready to roast.

Finally it was ready, a tender, delicious roast. And now came the time for the great Cleveland specialty – gravy. He poured the juice from the meat into a pot and stirred up a delicious fluid. I know, because I tasted it.

25

Quviasukvik- The Time for Rejoicing

—Alex Stevenson—

Alex Stevenson joined the Hudson's Bay Company as an apprentice trader in 1935 and was posted to Pond Inlet. After a long career with the Bay, he joined the federal government, eventually becoming Administrator of the Arctic for the Department of Northern Affairs, and Chairman of the Northwest Territories' Historical Advisory Board. In 1965 he wrote about his first Arctic Christmas for north *magazine.*

In December 1935 I had been at Pond Inlet for nearly four months as an apprentice fur trader in the service of "The Gentlemen Adventurers Trading Into Hudson's Bay" – Outfit 265 in a long history of trading. Here, five hundred miles inside the Arctic Circle at latitude 72°42' north lay the small settlement on the northeastern tip of Baffin Island – a rugged country of glaciers and mountainous coastline. The community consisted of the Hudson's Bay Company trading post, the Royal Canadian Mounted Police Detachment, and the Roman Catholic and Anglican Missions. Some three hundred Eskimo families from surrounding camps (including the people of Igloolik in Foxe Basin who in the spring would make a thousand-mile round trip) traded into Pond Inlet. But this was December and the supply ship which I had come North on, the *R.M.S. Nascopie,* our only link with the outside world, had made its annual visit in early September. We had not seen the sun for some time and the Arctic night with temperatures around thirty below had long ago settled in. Verdun, Quebec, my home town, was far away and I was rapidly adjusting to a new way of life. Among the many new things I was learning were how to bake bread, drive a dog team and repair harnesses and lines, shoot seals and narwhals, do book-keeping, and judge the quality of the white fox fur which was practically the sole medium of exchange used by the Eskimos in their dealings with the traders. I was also picking up something of the Eskimo language from trading supplies for pelts.

For days before Christmas I heard the cry: "*Qimussiq* – Dog team arriving." The people in the community shouted it to each other and turned out of their igloos to greet new arrivals from outlying camps who were coming to join in the celebrations. By Christmas Eve more than one hundred and fifty people had been added to the small settlement. The dog population had also increased to more than four hundred dogs, who would set up a howling chorus with the arrival of every new team or with the ringing of the mission bells.

Excitement and activity was all around. The men built snow houses, winter dwellings made of blocks of hard-packed snow, spiralling in the form of a dome. They moved their families inside and soon the *kudlik*, the seal oil soapstone lamp, that indispensable article in every Eskimo home, would be burning. Its wick of moss, trimmed by a capable woman, gave off a warm glow fairly free of smoke, and a white pleasant flame.

Many of the Eskimos gathered in the igloos to exchange tales of the hunt, their travels, births and deaths, and all the events that take place in the harsh life of these happy, courageous people.

Others came to the store to trade. Business went on by the light of coal oil or gasoline lanterns twenty-four hours a day. I wore a duffle cloth *koolituk,* or parka, in the unheated store and wrote out counterslips with stiff, cold fingers.

Several days before Christmas the company store turned baking supplies over to several Eskimo women so that preparations could be made for Christmas dinner. Four hundred pounds of flour were baked into bannock. Pots of beans with pork and molasses were prepared to be reheated at the last minute.

Northern foods – caribou steaks, Arctic hare and seal meat – rounded out the menu; a large barrel of hot, sweetened tea was steeped to be served on Christmas Day. Candy for the children, dress material for the women, and packages of tobacco for the men were set aside for distribution after the meal.

Christmas began officially on the evening of December 24 with midnight services at the missions. The two Royal Canadian Mounted Policemen wore the scarlet and gold; the missionaries put on their best cassocks; and my boss, a Scotsman and veteran Arctic trader who so often gave me wise counselling,

such as "Don't do as I do, laddie – do as I say," got out the suit of clothes he wore only at Christmas and ship time. I tried on my suit to discover that at nineteen I was still growing and the suit would not meet across my chest.

The Eskimos assembled with their hymn books, which were written in the syllabic script. They loved to sing and we could easily recognize the tunes of many well-known hymns.

On Christmas Day the Eskimo people moved into the ware-house for the feast. While they were feasting, I helped the post manager prepare dinner for our guests, the two policemen and the missionaries. I had baked fresh bread. A full-length Arctic char was broiling in a pan in the oven of the old black coal stove. Seal liver and caribou steaks simmered on the stove with a pot of dehydrated vegetables. Gaily painted menus had been made by one of the missionaries, who was extremely artistic. A mission also kindly donated wine for toasting the king and our families and friends so far away. For me the highlight of the meal was a tinned fruit cake that my mother had given me when we sailed from Montreal in July, with the loving request that it not be opened until Christmas.

After dinner, dog team races and games were held. About four miles out in the inlet two large icebergs were grounded or frozen in. We used to go out to them with the Post dog team and cut ice to be melted down for our water supply. It was decided that this would be the return point for the dog races. Teams were made up with from eight to sixteen dogs, depending largely on the resourcefulness of the owner and the extent of the hunting and trapping in his area. The sledges or *komatiks* were eighteen feet long or more, with spruce runners shod with steel or whalebone. Crossbars were tied on to the runners with seal thong. The runners were then iced to reduce friction. I noticed three Eskimos using the warmed blood of recently killed seals, ejecting it from their mouths on to the runners. It quickly congealed and water was then added and smoothed out with a piece of bearskin.

Fifteen teams lined up. A rifle shot rang out and the race was on. In the hazy light of the dark period they were soon out of sight but we could hear the calls of the drivers and the swish and crack of the whips followed by the howling and yelping of the wolf-like huskies. Normally these sturdy animals, each weighing from fifty to eighty pounds, would as a team pull *komatiks* carrying a thousand pounds on the trail all day; now with only a driver and a short distance to go – around the icebergs and back to land – it seemed no time until we could hear them coming back. Suddenly three teams almost neck and neck came flying along with Killitee, the Special Constable's team, making a final surge to win. Then the remaining teams rushed in and we were surrounded by fighting dogs, tangled lines, furry bodies rolling over and over in the snow, snarling and howling, Eskimos shouting and separating the fighters with whips and their boots. It appeared a hopeless tangle but with wonderful patience, the Eskimos soon had the various teams sorted out and driven to the snow houses for unharnessing.

In the evening an accordion and fiddle began to tune up in the crowded warehouse. Although the old Eskimo drum dances were still held in some Arctic settlements, the people of Pond Inlet preferred reels and jigs passed down from the early Scottish whalers. This area was frequented by whalers early in the 19th century and they continued to visit the Inlet until this century, when they were followed by the traders.

The dancing warmed up. Perspiration poured from the smiling faces. Many people wore caribou skins or duffle parkas throughout the dance; and they kept on their sealskin boots. Fun was the order of the day and everyone joined in. I am sure the frenetic urban dances of the south would be nothing compared to a few hours of Eskimo dancing in a crowded, close smoky room, dense with odors from skin clothing, and the noises of babies crying and men, women and children laughing and shouting. There are many intricate movements to the dance. The women appear to glide and shuffle their feet while the men do a tap and a jump, weave in and out and swing their partners. Up and down the room they move, round and round to the wild, weird, captivating rhythm of Scottish reels. Some of the women danced with babies on their backs.

I danced until every muscle of my body ached and still these amazing small people, whose ancestors probably trekked across the Arctic some two thousand years before Christ, kept on and on as if they would never tire.

For those of us from the south, Christmas night was the night for messages from home. We gathered round the radio. We had no transmitters, only a dry battery radio set that with luck would last the year. Throughout the winter the Canadian Broadcasting Corporation's Northern Messenger Service broadcasts personal messages weekly to the isolated residents in the Arctic from their families and friends Outside. These messages were dispatched in alphabetical order. Sometimes the announcer would only get halfway through the alphabet before time was up. Other times the program would fade out so that one could hardly keep from kicking the set. However, Christmas Night was a special occasion when arrangements had been made for across-Canada broadcasts. Friends and members of families were invited to CBC studios in various cities to convey greetings. My mother's voice came through clearly with a Scottish accent that took me a bit by surprise. I listened with nostalgia. It was the first of many Christmases I would spend in the North and other parts of the world, far from loved ones and friends at home.

Everyone from the oldest grandmother to the youngest baby was happily tired that night. All stomachs were full. The Eskimos bundled themselves in their caribou skin clothing and began to leave the warehouse, family by family. The lights in the settlement dimmed. The flickering stone lamps made a soft glow inside the snow houses that dotted the landscape. Overhead the northern lights streaked across the sky like a gigantic display of fireworks as if to commemorate the day the King of Kings was born.

The people of the Arctic had broken the monotony of the long winter night. *Quviasukvik* had come and gone for another year.

Warmth Beneath the Snow

Joseph P. Moody

Until the 1940s activities in the Canadian Arctic were dominated by the churches, the police and the traders. After the second world war all that changed with the gradual introduction of government services. Administrators, teachers, doctors and nurses came North in increasing numbers.

Joseph Moody, a physician, explorer and photographer, was one of the doctors who went North in the service of the Department of National Health and Welfare. He spent three and a half years in the Eastern Arctic among the Inuit at Chesterfield Inlet, from 1946 until 1949. In 1955 he published a record of his experiences in Arctic Doctor. *In it he described the effects of isolation and the early winter darkness on him and his family, effects which surprised and saddened him, for he had felt he would be able to cope well with his changed environment. He told of the deteriorating morale among the few white residents of the community and how, as the darkness of the Arctic days lengthened into the beginning of the Christmas season, people's spirits suddenly brightened.*

Fortunately, before our morale sank lower, the nearness of Christmas shed a more peaceful light over the community. According to those who had spent Christmas there before, the advance signs would be unmistakable.

One day we saw these signs for ourselves – strange Eskimo families appearing from nowhere and building their igloos among those of their brothers. Distant Eskimos, it seemed, always converged on the settlement before Christmas to share in the festivities. Their advent had a remarkable effect on the whites. Activities picked up: people moved about busily, driven by a real purpose for the first time in weeks. Wives were making candy and baking weird concoctions culled from well-thumbed cookbooks. Packages were being wrapped. Even the hobbyists were starting to turn out their masterpieces again.

The sudden restoration of a healthier outlook gave me vast relief. As a doctor, I had no wish to have more neurotic patients on my hands than is normal in the Arctic. Besides, I had been feeling too much that way myself to handle them with proper objectivity. Now everything looked better. The spirit of Christmas was in the air.

Viola felt better, too, and the baby, continuing to take things in her stride, was showing an appreciative interest in her surroundings. In fact, our daughter's increasing alertness to everything was really the cause of a new worry for me; a worry inadvertently suggested by a passing remark of Viola's three days before Christmas.

"I wish we could make a better Christmas for Gloria-May," she said. "More like the Christmas she'd have had in the South."
"So do I," I answered. "Well, she'll have some presents, anyhow."
"I wish, Joe," Viola continued, "we could have a – a *tree*."
"Tee, Daddy," lisped the small girl at her side.

A lump rose in my throat and I turned and stared out the window into the blackness. There wasn't a tree of any sort in this part of the land. The nearest scraggy evergreens were six hundred miles away!

Gloria-May had her Christmas tree after all – such as it was. The idea stayed in Viola's mind until her native ingenuity created a "tree" from the means at hand. Its backbone was a broomstick. For branches she fastened on small sticks and pipe cleaners, using tape. Then she covered the whole with strips of green crepe paper. Winter had either dulled or sharpened our imagina-

29

tions – I'm not sure which – but to us the result looked remarkably like a real tree. She had painted small light bulbs different colours, and these she and I hung in series on her masterpiece. There were tree ornaments, too, made out of cotton, wood and cardboard. When all was done, we set the contraption in front of the living room window, turned on the bulbs and let them stay lighted day and night.

Soon the fame of Viola's Christmas tree spread throughout the settlement. Several Eskimo children, completely awed by the display, spread the word to the others. In almost no time a path was beaten to our window where these little Eskimos stood for hours, their brown faces all smiles. Viola and I looked at each other. There was no need to say anything. The Christmas spirit was here.

On Christmas Eve a special party at the radio station served to carry on a traditional event of several years' standing. Similar Christmas Eve parties were being held in other Arctic settlements, their success depending largely on the fact that all were tied together by radio.

In Chesterfield the whites and a few Eskimos assembled in the tiny radio hut. Its atmosphere grew a bit thick, but all had a fine time. A special feature of this evening was permission to everyone to speak over the radio and send greetings to friends around the Arctic. Emotions were often controlled with difficulty, especially when voices began to be heard from the other posts. They seemed so near – yet actually they were so far away!

A program, broadcast by several gifted (more or less) members of our community, furnished needed diversity. Viola and one of the other women sang a duet. There were more duets and a solo or two. Some told their favorite stories. The nuns from the hospital had brought a small choir of Eskimo children, and it made us swallow hard to hear them sing carols and hymns in words they hardly understood but which held such deep meaning for us. Listening, we were only half-conscious of time or place, each sunk in his own thoughts.

Afterward it got gayer. One Eskimo played his mouth organ and another had brought his accordion. These furnished a decided change of pace. We also had records, and even swung into a few lively dances. Then the other radio stations made contact again, thanking us for our music and telling what was going on in their own little groups.

It was strange how those two or three hundred people who had chosen the Arctic for their home showed their awareness of this bond that united them. They lingered longingly around their far-flung microphones, loath, apparently, to break off the voices that came through the clear, cold skies.

Our party had a stabilizing, down-to-earth effect on all of us until, walking home, we were treated to a grandstand view of the Northern Lights, which undid it all.

I thought I knew what Northern Lights were like from watching their varied performances night after night. Though never the same, they followed a basic pattern of sorts – at least to the extent of accustoming you to a kaleidoscope of grandeur. But grandeur was hardly the word for what we saw in the heavens that night. I'm sure there never was a manifestation of more unbelievable beauty; the kind that enters your soul and does things to you. It started with a band of multicoloured light moving through the sky and finally rolling up into a tight ball. There were greens and reds and purples, soft yellows and oranges. As we looked, that ball of coloured fire grew bigger – *bigger* – *BIGGER! Then, with a noise that might have been a salvo from celestial artillery, it burst open, shooting out beams of light in the form of a giant star.*

Several moments passed before we could so much as *Oh*, or *Ah!* Then, as we turned toward home, someone murmured, in awed tones, "Star of Bethlehem."

The rest of the way Viola and I felt warm deep inside us; warm and very happy.

On Christmas Day, the mission put on its yearly "bean feast" for the Eskimos. It was exactly that – a festive occasion highlighted by the distribution of big bowls of cooked beans. How those Eskimos loved cooked beans! Just watching them eat was quite a sight. The recollection of other years had caused them to bring along a weird assortment of containers in which to carry away what could not possibly be eaten on the spot. This "gorge" led to considerable polite belching, and the whole affair culminated in square dancing – Eskimo style.

That evening all the whites of the settlement gathered at our home. We sat on the floor around Viola's improvised tree with the packages piled under it. She had made many different kinds of candy to munch on during the distribution of gifts. Everyone got a present of some kind which he or she pronounced "wonderful." But what excited everybody the most was opening the packages from home: the special presents, selected so many months in advance, that had finally reached us after their round-about, disaster-marked journey.

Earlier in the day we had brought over a small organ from the Hudson's Bay Company post. One of the mission Fathers now sat down at it and played until he had us joining in with our voices. Gradually the music faded out and we ended the evening with intimate talk of Christmases past. Somehow, it left us all quite happy with our little Arctic world.

From Christmas through New Year's was a high plateau in the Chesterfield calendar. Because there was something different doing every day, it would seem particularly foolish to lose any part of that lively period. Yet that's exactly what I did. I lost a day. It wasn't like the switching of days when you cross the date line: It was my own fault.

"Well, we're getting close to 1947," I happened to remark to Viola as we leafed through our day-by-day calendar.
"Tomorrow's the twenty-seventh."
"The twenty-eighth," she corrected.
"Twenty-seventh. This is Friday, isn't it?"

"*Friday?*" She looked at me as if I'd gone out of my senses. "Why, Joe, this is Saturday, the twenty-eighth, and you know it!"

To convince her she was wrong I went over to the radio hut for proof.

"This is Saturday, the twenty-eighth," they said, with a quick glance at their log to make sure.
"Then Viola is *right?*"
"Of course, Doc. Isn't she always?"

With a silly grin, I left them to go home and assure Viola that if either of us was off our reckoning, it wasn't she. I don't know yet where I mislaid that day. The continuous darkness probably was at the bottom of it.

ALLERSTON

Eskimo Christmas Tree

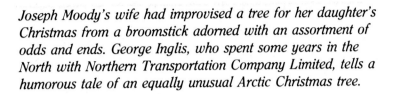

George Inglis

Joseph Moody's wife had improvised a tree for her daughter's Christmas from a broomstick adorned with an assortment of odds and ends. George Inglis, who spent some years in the North with Northern Transportation Company Limited, tells a humorous tale of an equally unusual Arctic Christmas tree.

Some years ago, at a lonely outpost on Canada's treeless Arctic coast, next door to Santa Claus land, one of the few white residents, homesick for Christmas festivities, decided to brighten things up with a Christmas tree. It was easier to think of than to accomplish.

Hearing of an Eskimo hunter about to travel South in search of caribou, the white man, through an interpreter, made his wish known to the Eskimo, who promised to bring him back a tree.

Just before Christmas Day, the smiling hunter returned across the snow with his sled loaded with caribou meat, and a fine, tall tree. Proudly, he pulled up before the waiting white man, who stared in speechless disappointment at the long, thick pole tied to the side of the sled.

To make things easier, and expedite his quick return with the promised tree, the Eskimo had lopped off all the branches.

Christmas at Aulatsivik

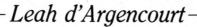

Leah d'Argencourt

Leah Idlout d'Argencourt is a bilingual Inuk woman who was born in northern Baffin Island. She now lives in Ottawa and is one of a growing number of Canadian Inuit who express themselves well to a wide public audience through the medium of English prose. In one of her articles she has recalled, from her youth, the simple joys of a Christmas season passed with her family at their hunting camp near Pond Inlet.

During the month before Christmas at Aulatsivik near Pond Inlet where our camp was situated when I was a child, the men would stay out trapping much longer than at any other time of year. Their purpose was to get enough white fox pelts to trade with the Hudson's Bay store. Also some of the men would be sent out by the camp leader to get enough fresh Arctic char, seal meat, *muktuk* (narwhal skin) from the cache, and caribou meat.

Even we youngsters would help to skin the foxes and clean them so they would be ready a few days before Christmas. The grandparents would have more fox skins than usual to dry and clean. This was really fun and it was enjoyable for everyone to be so busy. It was the first signal of the happy Christmas we were going to have.

In our camp it was not possible for all the members of the family to go Christmas shopping for gifts. This was done only by the men, who would go to the Hudson's Bay store in the settlement. It was always surprising to see the things they brought back with them, unusual gifts that included special *qadlunaat* food and machine-made clothing.

We had no Christmas trees in the camp, not even artificial ones. This was not because we were poor. It was just that there were none to be had at the Hudson's Bay store, and we didn't miss them.

A funny part of Christmas down South is that Santa Claus is supposed to come from the North Pole. I don't know which way he took on his way down South! We never saw him during my childhood, nor was he known by many Inuit children.

The night before Christmas, like children everywhere, we always had to go to bed before our parents so we would be bright and early getting up. The most important part was to rejoice and celebrate the birthday of our Lord Jesus Christ.

There is one Christmas I will never forget. That particular Christmas morning I woke up happy and feeling good to be with my loving parents. To my surprise they had hidden a Christmas gift between my duffle parka and the sealskin boots that I was sleeping on as a pillow. I don't know how my father or mother ever managed to hide it there without waking me up.

Merry Christmas! Merry Christmas! Merry Christmas! There must have been about eight of us sleeping on the sleeping platform. It was a cold, dark Christmas morning and I didn't want to be the first one to get up. But it was such a special morning and each child always tried to be the first one to be up and ready to go to the neighbours to shake hands with them.

Oops! I can't get my sealskin boots on, there is something sewn up in my duffle socks. It must be one of my darn brothers again! Oh, I just have to be the first one to be up and ready! What is the use of getting mad? It is such a special day. I made

ALLERSTON

it! I made it before them! Oops! There is something else, very cold, in the tip of my toe. Oh heck, what is it this time? The hard candies and the dried prunes are stuck to the caribou hair inside the skin feet of my duffle socks!

When I was finally ready, everybody was full of laughter. The next thing was to go to our grandparent's house. They were still so sleepy, they could hardly open their eyes, but their faces were warm and smiling. Merry Christmas! We shook hands on this very special day. Then we moved on to my cousin's house.

The day began with Christmas hymns at a morning gathering. Then we went on to playing games, and finally eating different kinds of cooked meat, and home-made beans and rice with raisins and powdered milk.

Even now, when it is getting close to Christmas time, I still often wonder where my father managed to find such unusual gifts for me and my brothers.

A very Merry Christmas to everyone!

35

Arctic Christmas

Richard Finnie

Richard Finnie was born in Dawson, Yukon Territory, and went on his first major Arctic expedition at the age of seventeen. He has been in and out of the North ever since, as explorer, filmmaker and photographer on numerous expeditions. Today he is over seventy years old and lives in California, yet he continues to visit the Arctic often. He spent the winter of 1930-31 in the central Canadian Arctic, and passed Christmas at the trading post of Coppermine.

When I was a small boy I read in one of my storybooks an account of the celebration of Christmas by Eskimos. It may have been satirical, but I accepted it as gospel. It told how these fur-clad folk ingeniously fashioned a tree out of whalebone and hung on it bon-bons of blubber for the children, how they all joined shiveringly in the singing of carols, how they huddled in icy igloos waiting in vain for Santa Claus. Though the old gentleman lived nearby he was too busy in more southerly climes to be able to deliver any presents to his neighbours. They had a pretty hard time of it and I felt very sorry for them.

Years passed, and then I suddenly recalled this childhood picture. Soon I would have an opportunity to make a comparison, for in a few days I myself would be celebrating Christmas among the Eskimos.

Dozens of families from the islands to the north, from capes and bays on the coast and from seal-hunting camps on the frozen sea, were on their way to Coppermine to hold a yuletide reunion. Until a few years ago, of course, these people had no knowledge of Christmas (my storybook notwithstanding), and in fact had no precise means of reckoning time whereby they could arrange to foregather on an appointed date. The influence of white men had altered this situation. Nearly every Eskimo family

now had a calendar upon which each day was carefully marked off; and they were aware at least in one respect of the significance of Christmas – it was a day of feasting and merrymaking for the whites, in which they too might join. And so their dogs were straining at the traces of sleds piled high with all manner of household goods, furs, seal oil and meat. While the adults broke trail and helped in harness with the dogs, the children rode on the sleds or pattered alongside.

Meanwhile the two religious missions were making ready special supplies of biscuits, jam and tea and other dainties to attract the natives to masses or services. The trading post manager was taking an inventory of his goods and getting the store in shape to do business. The doctor was determined to uphold at his hospital British Christmastide traditions as well as circumstances permitted. First of all, he wanted a Christmas tree. Such a thing had never been seen on the barren Arctic coast, but that did not deter him. He dispatched Kinuktuk with sled and dog-team, instructing him to proceed inland to the northern limit of wooded country, there to cut a spruce and bring it back to the settlement. The previous winter the doctor had ordered, through the Hudson's Bay Company, a collection of toys and candy which had subsequently been delivered in the open season by the annual supply ship. These he brought down from the attic and unpacked. On the following day Kinuktuk arrived from a non-stop trip to the interior. The tree he had picked out was symmetrical and of just the right height, and it became an object of amused curiosity when the doctor set it up in the living-room and decorated it with glass balls, festoons and candles.

Over at the wireless station, when not sending out weather reports to civilization, operators Fred Sealey and Peter Davies baked batches of bread and undertook mysterious culinary

experiments. They had issued a general invitation to the white colony for Christmas dinner.

By the twenty-fourth there were one hundred and thirty-nine Eskimos – men, women and children – assembled at the settlement. None of us had seen so many people at once for a long time. Theirs was a spirit of good fellowship; they joked and laughed and sang. While the women unloaded the sleds, the men set to work on the fringe of the sea-ice cutting blocks from the wind-packed snow and constructing commodious igloos.

In a few hours the igloos were habitable, furnished with deerskin bedding, numerous knick-knacks, and stone seal-oil lamps serving a three-fold purpose: heat, light and cooking. The Eskimos then started, according to a custom they had developed, to go the rounds of all the white men's dwellings, staying at each one long enough to enjoy some refreshments, mainly hardtack and tea.

To the Hudson's Bay Company's store the hunters brought their accumulated fox pelts – whites, crosses, silvers and reds. Post manager Barnes, good-humoured and patient, allowed his customers to deliberate as much as they wished over the choosing of goods, but tried to discourage too many purchases of golf sweaters, cheap jewelry, silk underwear and the like, recommending instead food, tools and ammunition as being more useful.

It was Christmas Day. The trading post apprentice had been prevailed upon to masquerade as Santa Claus. When the hospital was packed with guests, he made his entrance wearing a false beard and a conventional Santa Claus costume of scarlet flannel. The children screamed with fright, while the men and women drew back shyly to make way for this odd stranger. They had been told that a benevolent white man who lived much farther north than anyone else was to pay a call, but this man, they felt, could hardly be he. Why, he was not even wearing furs, though the temperature was forty degrees below zero, and his boots were not of moose-skin; this was not the proper attire for a dweller in the Far North! The impersonation lasted for

only a few minutes. Then the apprentice's beard half fell off and his face was recognized amid shouts of merriment. Undaunted, he began handing out the gifts: raisins and candy to everybody, pocket knives to the boys and, of all things, handkerchiefs to the girls.

A few of the whites who had come to the doctor's party were shortly captured by the spirit of revelry. Each of them persuaded a raven-haired fur-clad damsel to try a fox-trot with him as the radio was tuned to a static-free dance program from New York. The younger women, and even some of the more matronly ones carrying babies on their backs, seemed to have a sense of rhythm quite equal to that of any metropolitan debutante. An example having been set, the native men themselves were soon fox-trotting, executing a variety of steps that were original if not always graceful. And as they were all wearing moccasins, it really didn't matter if one trod on his partner's toes now and then.

Through the witchery of science we were all dancing to the latest Broadway tune.

At five o'clock when we entered the wireless station, our nostrils were assailed by a conglomeration of appetizing odours. It had been rumoured that the dinner was to be of exotic character, but no details had been learned. A menu was now displayed, and listed thereon were: *Potage* Ptarmigan, *Filet* of Arctic Salmon, Fried White Fox and Greenland Hare *a la King*, Roast Snowy Owl and Giblets of Seal, Caribou Steak, Canned Vegetables, Plum Pudding.

"We should consider ourselves especially privileged," chuckled Charlie Lewin. "What fancy restaurant anywhere in the world could duplicate this assortment?" The old Swedish trapper had journeyed from his lonely camp at the mouth of the Richardson River to spend Christmas with us.

The meal progressed splendidly until the final course, when the doctor ruefully directed attention to the absence of brandy to burn on the pudding. Astonished eyes were fixed upon him, for he was known to be an ardent teetotaler. "Well, what can we do about it?" he was asked. "So far as we know, there isn't a drop of anything stronger than ice-water around Coronation Gulf – but if there were, we'd have located it before now!"

"You can fool some of the people some of the time," he replied with a grin. "I should like to have every detail of this banquet as much as possible in keeping with old-country traditions. I have a bottle of brandy cached away. I'll fetch it."

He dashed out of doors amid chorused exclamations of: "So he's got a bottle of brandy!" . . . "I hope it's a big one!" . . . "Maybe it's going to be a merry Christmas after all!"

A few minutes afterward the doctor reappeared, flourishing a two-ounce bottle of the precious fluid, which he promptly emptied over the pudding and ignited.

One of the Eskimos brought word that a native dance was being held in the visitors' camp, and that we might attend if we cared to. Believing it would provide a striking contrast to our own festivities, we made our way toward the cluster of dome-shaped structures dotting the shoreline. Yellow light from seal-oil lamps shone cheerily through ice windows, and as we drew nearer we could hear the weird throbbing of a drum.

Gathered in an enormous igloo, men and women began the ceremony by forming a circle and humming softly while one of them stepped into the centre and thumped a drum to test its pitch. (The Eskimos' only musical instrument is a light wooden hoop over which caribou skin is tightly stretched.) Holding it in his left hand by a short handle, he then swung it from side to side against a club in his other hand as he danced and sang. The dance had no set form but was often the pantomimic compliment of the songs. Some of the songs were composed on the spot, others seemed to be well known to nearly everybody. The themes dealt with simple incidents in the lives of the people, or extolled the prowess of this or that hunter. When not taking turns with the drum, the Eskimos kept in the circle and chanted the choruses.

Though we could understand hardly a word of the songs, the spectacle held us enthralled for several hours. There was something mysterious and compelling in its simplicity and rhythm. Aware that this dance had been presented in much the same way for thousands of years, we soberly reflected that in a little while hence it would probably disappear – swallowed up by the white man's invading culture.

The igloos were abandoned the next day. The visitors packed all their belongings on their sleds, and with staccato commands to their teams ringing out in the crisp air they drove off into the distance. The settlement was left quiet and forlorn.

ALLERSTON

Operation Santa Claus

Margery Hinds

In the 1940s the federal government launched Operation Santa Claus to deliver the Christmas mail to isolated posts in the Canadian Arctic as a means of making the winter's isolation more bearable to southerners in the service of government in the North. The Royal Canadian Air Force air-dropped mail – and a Christmas tree – to each community at the time of the last full moon before Christmas. The program was discontinued in 1967, by which time transportation to the Arctic had improved.

Margery Hinds was one of the first school teachers in Baffin Island. An adventurous and unattached woman, she had already lived among Lapps and Maoris before teaching in Arctic Quebec, the Mackenzie District and Baffin Island. In her book, High Arctic Venture, she described the excitement of the Christmas mail drop in the winter dark at Arctic Bay, where she lived with her inseparable companion, her dog Pingua, "the plaything." She told also of the satisfaction of organizing the first school Christmas concert in the village.

One day in December when I was getting Avinga's cake of earth, news came by radio that the Christmas mail plane was on its way. More camp Eskimos than usual were in the village at this time as they had picked up news of the date of the Christmas drop on their radios. Although they didn't speak English, some had a smattering acquired in hospital. All Eskimos understood dates and had calendars. They listened to the special Eskimo broadcasts transmitted by the Canadian Broadcasting Corporation, which included news items of interest to Arctic residents. Thus, many of the men arranged their visits to the trading post to coincide with the mail drop.

So when it was time to light the flares, there were many willing helpers. There were plenty of sleds and dog teams, too, for collecting the big hampers and parachutes as soon as the plane had continued its journey.

That square on the bay was indeed a cheerful sight when all the flares were flickering on the oil drums. It seemed that a well-lighted little town had appeared by magic in the middle of the frozen sea.

Suddenly, blood-curdling howls rent the silence. All the dogs began to wail. Their ululations informed us that the aircraft was approaching, though we human beings could hear nothing. It was indeed a welcome sound to all who had congregated out of doors in the thirty-five degrees below zero weather. Eskimos were the next to hear the plane's engines, and shortly afterwards the faint hum became audible to the white people too. I wondered what other senses of white people had become dulled by civilization.

Some moments later, the red and green lights of a flying boxcar appeared above the distant hills, and in a matter of seconds, the plane was circling round to drop two parachutes.

Although the drop took place during the lightest part of daytime darkness, had it not been for flashlights at the end of each hamper, we should not have seen them descend. Only the speed of the descent told us that the parachutes had opened, for we could not see them. Some of us had ordered fragile articles from a store in Toronto, and hoped they would not be smashed to smithereens.

"Only two parachutes!" someone commented. "Is that all?" Anxious eyes peered into the darkness to watch the lights on the aircraft. It was circling again. This time three more hampers were dropped. Then something came down very fast, with no parachute.

"That's the Christmas tree!" one of the children said, gleefully.

"That's all. The Christmas tree always comes last," a local Eskimo mother told her small children, who wanted to see more little lights come out of the plane.

By that time, the lamps of the magic village had gone out and the aircraft was on its way to the next settlement some hundreds of miles away. The Arctic Bay drop had been perfect. Everything landed inside the square of lights and every parachute had opened. The few twigs which broke off the wrapped Christmas tree were fixed on again with wire.

The Christmas tree, which was not part of the mail, was a gift from the men of the Royal Canadian Air Force, who donated trees to all the tiny, remote settlements far above the tree-line.

As there were flashlights on the hampers, and everything had landed in the target area, there was no difficulty in finding the items. And because one end of the landing square had been left open, no time was lost because of dog lines becoming entangled round oil drums. Thus, one by one, the *komatiks* returned without delay to Hudson's Bay House for the mail to be sorted by the acting postmaster – a job which I had had in one of my posts. But first, the parachutes were removed from the hampers and folded up ready to be returned with the hampers to the post office at ship time.

The following year, the drop was made during the evening, and that time I helped with the sorting. That year, the weather was so cold on mail day, that those who unbuckled the parachutes with their bare hands acquired small spots of frostbite on the tips of their fingers. But instead of complaining, they made jokes about it.

Hampers were carried into the porch, where Eskimos emptied them of numerous bags of mail which they took into the kitchen. The two Scots and I took one bag at a time into the large attractive living room that became a temporary sorting office. The letters, parcels and magazines that came out of the bags were so cold that soon my fingers began to freeze. Every now and again, I stopped sorting to go to the kitchen to warm my hands in the oven.

Once, when the assistant manager was sorting parcels, he exclaimed, "Lucky dog," then, handing me a parcel said, "Just look at that!"

The parcel was directed to Mr Pingua, c/o Miss Hinds. It was from a lady in Ottawa whose guest he had once been while I was overseas on leave. Since that time he had received a parcel from her every Christmas. There were also letters and parcels for Eskimos from their friends and relatives in hospital in southern Canada, or from those engaged in wage employment in other parts of northern Canada. The letters were written in the syllabic script, but of course, the envelopes were addressed in Roman characters.

One of the hampers was so heavy that it took several people to lift it into the porch.

"I can guess what's in this one," one of the schoolboys said, as soon as he began taking out the bags. "Yes," he exclaimed, "it's full of movie films!" It was.

A hamper which was only partially full of mail, had the rest of the space filled with used paperbacks and magazines which personnel of the RCAF had collected and sent along as an act of kindness. The Services stationed in the North get mail frequently and regularly, and sometimes they show their solicitude for civilians in the isolated places by including used reading matter in the mail drop.

Eventually, the sorting was finished and the erstwhile tidy living room at Hudson's Bay House looked as though it had been struck by a tornado. Eight big sacksful of mail for me were loaded on a *komatik* and dragged to the house by several lads.

Now another sorting had to be done, but before attempting it, I followed my usual practice on mail day by giving refreshments to those who had helped. In quite a short while, after all the cakes were eaten and the coffee pots empty, the Eskimos went away.

Now Pingua began cleaning the floor of crumbs while I hurriedly washed dishes and made space available on tables, chairs and the floor. Every square inch of room would be needed for sorting mail. At last I tipped out the contents of the first sack. Then, sitting beside it, I flung it into piles in various parts of the room – personal, official, school, magazines, parcels, and finally, junk. The junk was mainly unwanted advertisements which manufacturers call educational material; presumably for educating the public to use their products. A very limited amount of it was of use, though seldom in the way intended by the senders.

The Eskimos who lit the flares and collected the hampers and parachutes on mail day started the return journey to their camps the following day. Their next visit to the village would be at Christmas, when their wives and families would come too. All of them would be wearing something new to celebrate the festive season.

By the time the men reached home, the women had almost finished the Christmas sewing. On the hand-driven Singer sewing machine they had stitched dresses of gay cotton print, and plain-coloured *silapas* – windproof covers for parkas. Other materials which they had bought at ship time had been made into parkas and Arctic stockings, but these were sewn by hand, as the special kind of seam used on thick woollen blanket cloth cannot be done by machine.

Original designs of colourful wool embroidery decorated the parkas and the tops of the Arctic stockings; and rows of bright braid or rick-rack were sewn on the *silapas*.

In a few homes there were white fox skins which were unacceptable to the trader because ravens, gyrfalcons or snowy owls had torn them almost to ribbons. But girls, with much patience, had sewn them together, and would use them for trimming the hoods of their parkas. Girls who had no white fox used the winter coat of the Arctic hare, a fur of no commercial value.

When the Christmas sewing is finished, women and girls look at the new garments with satisfaction and relief. They put them into large, washed flour bags ready to be packed on the *komatik* with the travelling gear when they set out on the long journey to the village of Arctic Bay for Christmas.

Men, too, have to make their Christmas preparations. It is their responsibility to supply the food. In the Eskimo language food is synonymous with meat. There must be enough dog food to last until they return home again. Frozen walrus or narwhal must be fetched from the caches and chopped into bite-sized pieces, then packed in sacks. Food for the family's round trip and for the stop-over at the settlement, usually frozen Arctic char and seal meat, must be got ready. And there must be food to offer as presents to those in whose homes they will stay during the Christmas holiday. Perhaps there will also be a fish or a seal liver for the teacher and the traders. If the Eskimo offers such things as a gift, he will receive a gift of the recipient's own choosing. But if he trades them, he will expect to receive whatever he requests, probably tea or sugar. There is an unwritten law in the Arctic – food for food – an item of food is exchanged for food of another kind.

While preparations were being made for Christmas, any spare time of men, older boys, and even of some women, was taken up with carving handicrafts. In past years enough white foxes had usually been caught before Christmas for the trapper to get whatever he needed from the store, but this was a bad year for foxes, and to supplement their income, many Eskimos began to make carvings, as those in other regions had been doing for several years.

ALLERSTON

The same sort of activity took place in every camp until it was time to set out on the long journey. Each group of people planned to reach the village in time for the young folk to attend the children's party in the school; it was the very first children's party there had ever been at Arctic Bay.

Each family already knew in whose home they would be staying. With so many people coming to the village from camps, and so few permanent residents at Arctic Bay, the tiny wooden houses of the local Eskimos were soon full to over-flowing. At bedtime, every square inch of floor space was occupied by visitors in their sleeping bags, and in all the beds there were more than the usual number of people.

Surely the Christmas story, of the long journey, of no room at the inn, and of bright lights of herald angels singing in the sky, needed no explaining to these Eskimos, especially if the Northern Lights had accompanied them on their journey.

Even with such overcrowding, there was never enough room in the homes of local Eskimos for all the visitors to find sleeping space. Some were obliged to build igloos.

Igloos made of snow have never been used as family homes in this part of the Arctic. Until the Eskimos had wooden houses, the winter homes were made of rocks and turf, and lined with the tent they used in summer. But they used igloos as temporary accommodation, and still do. An igloo for the night consists of one dome and sometimes a tiny entrance porch. It can be put up in about one hour by an experienced builder.

The younger ones among my regular pupils, who had always lived in the village, had never slept in an igloo, because they had never made a long journey in winter. They were fascinated.

Careful planning of feeding arrangements and games was necessary, as the classroom, twenty feet by sixteen feet, was far too small to accommodate comfortably all who came, for there were teenagers above school age and tiny tots too, in addition to all the others. But the school was the only suitable place in the village.

I had lived among Eskimos long enough to know what they liked to eat, and had included in my personal food order enough for the party and for entertaining the numerous visitors who would pay social calls at Christmastime.

Preparations occupied several weeks, but thanks to the intensely cold weather, it was possible to cook some things in advance, and freeze them until required. Cakes, pies, cookies and bread rolls, frozen immediately after baking, are almost like freshly baked food when they are quickly thawed just before eating.

Many Eskimos are good organizers where the best use of limited space is concerned, and the children were accustomed to fitting themselves into small places. There was no noise or confusion in the schoolroom about seating the crowd of guests. All the furniture had been put out of doors or into the porch to leave the floor space clear. To seat them all, so that food could be served, they joined hands and made three rings, the tiniest in the centre ring and the big ones in the outer ring. Then they sat and unclasped hands.

Dishes of food were in the centre of the room, and a narrow pathway was left between them and the porch door. A few big children helped with serving. Nothing whatever was spilled.

The main item on the menu, and a favorite dish of many Eskimos, was stew! It was made with canned ingredients: meat, vegetables and soup, to which cooked macaroni was added.

We were just about to serve second helpings of stew – the first course on the menu – when there came a loud knock at the door. Suddenly the thought of Santa Claus came to mind. Few, if any, Eskimos here had ever heard of the old fellow and there seemed to me no point in teaching about him. If I tried to explain in the English language no one would have understood, and if I used the Eskimo tongue, there would be the difficulty of finding words in that language that would correctly put across the idea of Santa Claus. It had been puzzling enough to explain the Christmas tree. Besides, Santa Claus belongs to the culture of a certain group of western peoples, and at that stage in

Eskimo education it seemed to me undesirable to load young minds with fables.

So, although the loud knocking at the door reminded *me* of Santa Claus, no one else had such a thought. From the loudness of the knocking I judged that a very big person was there. When I opened the door I saw what looked like a cuddlesome toy. It was a little Eskimo boy dressed in a hooded caribou-skin suit. Just visible among the fur was a small part of a face glowing red with cold, and in which two black eyes sparkled. This three-year-old seemed to be quite alone, but as soon as I took his hand to bring him into the schoolroom, his father appeared from behind the porch door.

After all the stew and all the pies and cakes had been eaten, the bigger children helped tidy the room and carry pots and dishes to the porch.

They played musical bumps, pass the parcel, musical arms, and fox's tail – a fox being more appropriate than a donkey! They danced and they sang, until most of the small children were fast asleep upon the floor and the party ended.

The program for Christmas Day at Arctic Bay was practically the same as that of other small Arctic communities. The Eskimos began by putting on their fine new clothes and going to the school for a church service which they conducted themselves in their own language, according to the order of services in the Book of Common Prayer of the Anglican Church. They sang the usual Christmas hymns of that church, using the same tunes to a translation of the words into Eskimo. Their church books are written in the Eskimo syllabic script.

There had been no missionary resident in the district since the death of Canon Turner at Moffet Inlet thirteen years previously, yet these Eskimos were more devout in their religious observances than people who have been educated in church schools and who live in parishes with resident parsons. The Arctic missionaries of the early days did a good job, generally speaking. Apparently they used a good deal of hellfire and brimstone as teaching aids, but by all accounts they were good-living, decent, honest men who were sincere in their work.

After the morning service, many of the Eskimos paid visits at my house and at the traders'. Others congregated with their friends in various Eskimos' homes until it was time for the community feast. This was provided by the Hudson's Bay Company, and took place in a warehouse that had been emptied of merchandise and specially heated. This building was larger than the school, but it was much too small to accommodate everyone comfortably, though somehow we all managed to squeeze in.

After the feast there were dog team races, with the prizes for the winning teams donated by the traders, and the booby prize of a pound of tea, offered by me. It was extremely cold weather, and so dark that even when the dogs were near they were scarcely visible. So, as I was to cook Christmas dinner to which the traders had been invited, I went home to prepare it. (They, being Scots, celebrated New Year's Day and invited me to their dinner party.)

In honour of Christmas, and for the first time that year, I put on a dress. Pingua evidently mistook it for a nightie, and promptly went to his sleeping place!

We ate dinner while the Eskimos were having their Evensong church service. During the meal, mention was made of radio programs and of the Christmas messages to Northern residents. Not one of us had remembered to listen; we had been far too busy, and had missed them all. I wondered whether, as usual, they had been addressed to the *men* of the North. One would suppose that no women lived there!

We had scarcely finished dinner when the church service ended and people began calling at the house again. The visits were brief, as it was almost time for the next item on the program, movies in the school. Some of the films had arrived by air-drop,

and included one of an Eskimo legend, "Kumak, the Sleepy Hunter," which was cleverly acted by puppets, and greatly enjoyed by the Eskimos of Arctic Bay.

Eskimo scenes that I had filmed in northern Quebec also created great interest. Just for fun, when editing these shots, I had inserted between two sections of Eskimos hunting a piece of film showing polar bears at Skansen Zoo, Sweden. A roar of laughter arose when the bears appeared on the screen. Afterwards they asked where I had seen those bears.

"You must know someone who keeps bears as pets," they said. "Bears simply don't behave like that!"

I confessed, and they were pleased that they hadn't been fooled.

After the film show there was a dance in the Company's warehouse. But before the dancing began, many people went to wherever they were staying to make tea, and those who were to play the dance music fetched their accordians and mouthorgans.

It was a long time before dancing was in full swing. Everyone seemed too shy to be first to begin. Sporadically, dancing continued throughout the night. A few were still dancing at breakfast time, though most of them were then in their sleeping-bags, where they remained all day long, or what is called day during the dark season.

When they awoke, some came to that evening's film show in the school. Others, who had arrived from distant camps on December twenty-third, and who had finished their trading before the store closed for the Christmas holiday, decided to start on the homeward journey. The weather was clear. Hard-packed snow squeaked underfoot, indicating good travelling conditions. Several hundred loose dogs were roaming around the village, and it was a wonder the owners of the teams could find them. But they did.

Christmas in the Big Igloo

Frank S. Gonda

Pelly Bay is one of the most isolated and traditional communities in the Canadian Arctic. Frank Gonda taught school there in the early 1960s, and described for north *magazine the highlight of the festive season there – the celebration of Christmas in the large communal snow house constructed each year specifically for that purpose.*

Once again last year the traditional snow house or *kaget* was erected in Pelly Bay for the Yuletide festivities.

The Big Igloo was built over three smaller igloos. These three snow houses serve as temporary homes for the family group who live about twenty miles from Pelly Bay, but always come to the settlement for Christmas. These people arrived in a blizzard on a Wednesday, December 19th, and immediately their igloos were established close to the mission.

On Saturday practically everyone turned out to cut and haul snow-blocks – women and children shovelled soft snow over the snowhouse for added insulation. On Monday the last block was put in. The inside was then cleared out and the three little snow houses over which the *kaget* was built were literally sliced in half, so that what remained was a big igloo about twenty-five feet in diameter and fifteen feet in height. Added space was created by the small igloos which were now raised alcoves; all that remained of the original igloos were the sleeping platforms. These alcoves made ideal balconies from which to view the festivities, and were the favourite places for the older men and women of the settlement. The platforms were covered with caribou robes and made still more comfortable and cosy by the *kudlic*, which was always lit. An important feature of the snow house was the porch, about six feet high. One entered on hands and knees through the entrance of minimum dimensions.

At eight o'clock Christmas Eve, one hundred and five gaily attired men, women and children assembled in the igloo for what was to be three nights and two days of games, contests, feasting and prayers.

Christmas Eve was highlighted by ancient Eskimo games and target shooting. Firing from about twenty-five feet with a .22 at strings from which dangled various prizes was quite a feat of marksmanship. A few of the contestants miraculously hit a string and thus claimed a prize. A special moment of Christmas Eve was the opening of presents. These gifts were sent to Father Van de Velde from his sister in Belgium. There was a gift for everyone. Such practical objects as cloth, wool, knives and even chess sets were the most frequent items. The Eskimos here are avid chess players.

Midnight Mass, said by Father Van de Velde, was solemn and beautiful, and somehow, having this service in an igloo seemed to bring the message that is Christmas so vividly to everyone.

After Mass, we enjoyed a lunch prepared by the mission and consisting of tea, porridge and biscuits. Candies were distributed to the children.

Christmas day was extremely cold. The thermometer read 48 degrees below zero when everyone came to the igloo at eleven-thirty for Mass. After Mass everyone went home for awhile to wait for the big Christmas dinner at three o'clock. The stew had been cooking slowly all night, and needed last-minute attention before serving up.

At three o'clock everyone converged on the igloo again, bringing mugs with them. Dinner was ready. The first course was sixty frozen Arctic char, previously sliced. After this was put away, the two huge kettles of caribou stew were brought in. Mugs were

dipped in and soon this too disappeared. Then the steaming kettles of tea were brought in. Each family brought its kettle; there were about twenty-five one-gallon kettles full of lovely, strong, hot tea. Needless to say each was drained.

After dinner there were more games, contests, prizes and candy. The archery contest was performed with an ancient bow of musk-ox horn. Each contestant shot four arrows from about fifteen feet. The target was an iron ring about two inches in diameter stuck in the igloo wall. Practically everyone had a turn, beginning with the oldest hunter. The last to try were the small children, and even the women took part.

In some ways the day after Christmas was the most exciting. We moved out of the igloo for some of the events. The feature event was the dog team race. Twenty-seven drivers and one hundred and sixty-two howling dogs took part; each driver was allowed six dogs. It was very cold and the course was long; many of the Eskimos had donned their caribou parkas.

The start was furious. Many teams got tangled, momentarily, but everyone was straightened away, and soon disappeared into the gloom across Pelly Bay. The winner, Otto Apsaktauk, returned over the course in about forty minutes, closely followed by Augustin Annartok. The rest soon returned to claim their prizes. Each was eligible. Twenty-seven prizes were placed on a table, and each in turn, according to his position in the race, stepped up to claim a prize. The prizes were good, but, of course, the big prize was winning the race, for this would be remembered, and would be a topic of conversation until the next race.

Other outdoor events included the foot races, and one marvelled at the endurance of the Eskimos in being able to run in such extreme cold. One was for the young men, who ran to the top of a hill about one and one half miles from the Mission and back. The hill is about one thousand feet high and there is a huge cross on top. Every contestant was awarded a prize – with the winners getting first choice.

At five o'clock it was back in the *kaget* for the drum dance. One seemed to be transported back to ancient times listening to the aged ladies chanting their weird songs and hearing the boom of the drum and watching the dancer gyrate to the rhythm of the beat. The dancer would emit an occasional *"Iy-hi"* which added more strangeness to the atmosphere. In each of the alcoves there were five or six chanters, and these ladies would sing the song of the dancer, whatever it was. It might be the Song-of-my-Father or the Song-of-my-Grandfather. The drumming and chanting stopped at 10 P.M., and soon everyone went home. That is how we celebrate Christmas in Pelly Bay.

ALLERSTON

Christmas in Hunting Camp

Atsainak Akeeshoo

The celebration of Christmas in a hunting camp was recalled in 1974 by Atsainak Akeeshoo, a young Inuk woman, raised in a camp, who had moved to the modern community of Frobisher Bay.

We had Christmas in hunting camps too, remember?

On Christmas morning, we would all get up very early in the morning, go to our neighbours' houses and shake everybody's hands.

Then we would wait all day for it to get dark so we could start exchanging gifts with friends and the adults. We would give away needles, pieces of rope, perhaps five bullets for father, marbles, thread and even our clothing that we've been wearing for years. Each of these things became treasures, like a multi-million dollar diamond would be to rich people.

Dog teams would come to our camps bearing gifts from the other camps and we would return their visit in the same way. There was no feasting but everyone got into gift-giving as if it was going to be the last Christmas ever.

Our mothers would receive bags, donated by churches, each containing thread, thimble, needles, face cloth or towel, and a bar of face soap. It was so exciting to see all those nice-smelling things come out of the bags one by one! Each piece was looked at and felt by all the members of the household before we went on with the rest.

If we were lucky, we would each get two pieces of candy or gum and maybe even a hard biscuit. Sometimes the RCMP used to come, by dog team, just before Christmas and they would leave a whole box of biscuits and that would be saved till Christmas night.

Christmas was not at all commercialized then. We celebrated the birth of Christ and followed what the three wise men did on Christmas night. Christmas was not for Santa Claus and toys and free candies. There was a form of a Santa Claus, a gift-giver, but we weren't taught to believe in him. I wonder how many children know about our old Christmas days and how much fun they can be without all kinds of treats in schools, big community parties for children with cartoons and free gifts from the government?

Today, the children rely on Santa Claus to make their Christmas a happy time with tinsel and gifts. We still have a gift-giving or exchanging but it doesn't get into a fever-pitch like it used to. We have feasts with turkey and cranberries and plum pudding, just like the missionaries taught us to.

Why not try to bring the old spirit of Christmas back this year so we can overflow with happiness . . . Inuit and Whites exchanging gifts and going into each others' homes to wish each other a Merry Christmas!

Community Christmas
Alooktook Ipellie

Alooktook Ipellie is a talented Inuk author and artist from Frobisher Bay. He now lives in Ottawa. In an article from north/nord *magazine in 1972 he describes succinctly and eloquently Christmas in a Northern community.*

The celebration of Christ's birthday was probably first introduced to the Eskimos by the early missionaries who came to preach the word of God to the inhabitants of the Arctic. As the years went by, the white man's way of celebrating Christmas was gradually adopted by the Eskimo. Now, the Eskimo follows Christmas in much the same way as the white man – which isn't surprising since he learned it from him.

An important festivity of the week is the traditional community feast. The menu consists of caribou, seal or Arctic char with tea and bannock. The food is served buffet-style, steaming hot, in large pots to a long line of hungry people. It's a happy get-together where everyone knows one another and there is much laughing, talking, and smiling.

Dances are held every night during the week. Music is usually provided by a number of ladies playing the accordion; as one tires, another replaces her. Everyone joins hands – they sway and swing, around and back again. The whooping merry sounds are heard throughout the night.

The Eskimo dances are like big square dances where you can have any number of pairs in a single circle as long as the four sides are equal. Each round lasts from a good half hour to a full hour. When the music finally stops, the dancers rush out the door, looking like hot kettles as they move into the cool air, perspiration steaming from their bodies.

After much dancing and gift exchanging, (gifts are exchanged throughout the season, from the twenty-fifth to the thirty-first of December) comes New Year's Eve – the time for Eskimo games to begin. All male adults are welcome to play in the games. Participants and onlookers form a large circle. The director of the games stands in the middle. He has a list of the games to be played and directs the entire program, making sure everyone can see. He announces the game to be played and gives a demonstration to make it clear to everyone.

It takes two people to start a game. One person enters the circle, indicating that he wants to try his luck and then waits for a challenger. But you have only one chance! If you lose, you can't play the game anymore. In order to become champion you must remain undefeated until no one else will challenge you.

The last of the festivities is celebrated on January first, New Year's Day. It's a time when dog team and, more recently, snowmobile races are held. Anyone is eligible to enter for a small fee that goes towards the prizes. At times the weather is cold and biting but that never dulls the excitement or stops the spectators from coming and cheering their favourite driver. The echoes of laughing sounds, stomping sounds, whooping sounds and engine sounds keep coming back to my mind.

Sources

Christmas at Winter Harbour, from William Edward Parry, *Journals of the First, Second and Third Voyages for the Discovery of a North-West Passage . . .*, London: John Murray, 1828.

Good Humour and Merriment on a Christmas Day, from George Francis Lyon, *The private journal of Captain G. F. Lyon, of H. M. S. Hecla, during the recent voyage of discovery under Captain Parry*, London: John Murray, 1824.

We Kept Christmas Well and Long, from Otto Sverdrup, *New Land; Four Years in the Arctic Regions*, New York: Longmans, Green, 1904.

A Horrible Mockery of the Spirit of Christmas, from Charles Edward Smith, *From the Deep of the Sea*, London: A & C Black Ltd., 1922.

Christmas in the High Arctic, from Joseph-Elzear Bernier, *1) Report on the Dominion Government Expedition to Arctic Islands and the Hudson Strait on Board the C. G. S. "Arctic" 1906-1907*, Ottawa: King's Printer, 1909; *2) Report on the Dominion Government Expedition to the Northern Waters and Arctic Archipelago of the D. G. S. "Arctic" in 1910*, Ottawa; Government of Canada, n.d.

We Did Not Pass a Very Merry Christmas, from Alfred Tremblay, *Cruise of the Minnie Maud*, Quebec: Arctic Exchange and Publishing Ltd., 1921.

Christmas in the Wilderness, from Leslie H. Neatby (ed.), *My Life Among the Eskimos: The Baffinland Journals of Bernhard Adolph Hantzsch, 1909-1911*, Saskatoon: University of Saskatchewan, 1977.

That First Christmas Day in Baffin Land, from Archibald Lang Fleming, *Archibald the Arctic*, New York: Appleton-Century-Crofts, Inc., 1956.

The Feast of Sedna, Anonymous, *north*, vol. XVI, no. 6, Nov.-Dec. 1969, p. 13.

Christmas Time in Northern Labrador, Sam Metcalfe, *Inuktitut*, Winter 1978, pp. 18-26.

A Little Drink to Fortify Himself, from Dagmar Freuchen (ed.), *Peter Freuchen's Adventures in the Arctic*, New York: Julian Messner Inc., 1960.

Quviasukvik — The Time for Rejoicing, from Alex Stevenson, "Arctic Christmas — Thirty Years Ago," *north*, vol. XII, no. 6, Nov.-Dec. 1965, pp. 28-31.

Warmth Beneath the Snow, from Joseph P. Moody, *Arctic Doctor*, New York: Dodd, Mead and Company, 1955.

Eskimo Christmas Tree, George Inglis, *north*, vol. XV, no. 6, Nov.-Dec. 1968, p. 44.

Christmas at Aulatsivik, from Leah d'Argencourt, "Merry Christmas!", *Inuit Today*, vol. 5, no. 11, Dec. 1976, pp. 28-40.

Arctic Christmas, from Richard Finnie, *Lure of the North*, Philadelphia: David McKay Company, 1940.

Operation Santa Claus, from Margery Hinds, *High Arctic Venture*, Toronto: Ryerson Press, 1968.

Christmas in the Big Igloo, Frank S. Gonda, *north*, vol. X, no. 6, Nov.-Dec. 1963, pp. 28-29.

Christmas in Hunting Camp, Atsainak Akeeshoo, *Inukshuk*, 23 Dec. 1974, p. 8.

Community Christmas, Alooktook Ipellie, *north/nord*, vol. XIX, no. 6, Nov.-Dec. 1972, pp. 24-27.

Other titles from
Outcrop
The Northern Publishers
Box 1350
Yellowknife, Northwest Territories, Canada
X1A 2N9

Great Bear: A Journey Remembered
Frederick B. Watt

NWT Data Book
Marina Devine, ed.

Plant Magic for Northern Gardens
Chriss D. Briggs

On Blue Ice: The Inuvik Adventure
Jane Stoneman-McNicol, ed.

Rebels, Rascals and Royalty:
The Colourful North of LACO Hunt
ed. Barbara Hunt